*Praise for*

# THE EDUCATION OF A YOUNG POET

"Woven throughout the memoir are inspiring anecdotes about leading a literary life, including insights into the craft of writing and the power of language in everyday life and in literature."　　　　—*Poets & Writers*

"As a match newly struck, *The Education of a Young Poet* recovers a dream-like glow of this world . . . The author's journey restores our sense of the visionary power of language."　　　　—*The Carolina Quarterly*

"I love the scope of *The Education of a Young Poet*, which opens fifty years before the author's birth. What better way of expressing the idea that poetry, like all art, is a matter of lineage, growing in equal part out of what we learn and who we are? Indeed, what David Biespiel has in mind here is less a craft book—although there are great craft riffs—than a memoir, a kind of portrait of the artist as a young man. 'Feeling alien within the familiar,' Biespiel describes it, the sensation of being a new poet. It's as good a description as I've seen for the mix of distance and proximity, alienation and empathy, that all art requires, and perhaps most especially that of poetry."
—DAVID L. ULIN, author of *Sidewalking*

"What a memorable, companionable, and singular book. I can't think of another contemporary memoir that has this mix of political and literary intelligence, all embedded in a personal story that is told with great candor, historical consciousness, and wit. How I wish it had existed when I was a young poet!"
—CHRISTIAN WIMAN, author of *Hammer Is the Prayer*

"Whether he is writing about poetry, politics, competitive diving, or the glories of great conversation, Biespiel's recurring subject is the tension between freedom and discipline—between the sublime release of our own wildness and the precision that comes only from exquisite self-control. Part memoir, part ars poetica, *The Education of a Young Poet* is a feast: of language, of memory, and of insights into how one young writer came into his own."    —PATRICK PHILLIPS, author of *Blood at the Root* and *Elegy for a Broken Machine*

"Lyrical, affectionate... Graceful reflections on creativity."
—*Kirkus Reviews*

"Biespiel's memoir delivers with wit and intelligence exactly the kind of inspiration any young writer requires: A voice and a past and a story to tell."
—*Empty Mirror*

# THE
# EDUCATION
# OF A
# YOUNG
# POET

# THE EDUCATION OF A YOUNG POET

## DAVID BIESPIEL

COUNTERPOINT PRESS

BERKELEY, CALIFORNIA

The Education of a Young Poet

The Library of Congress has cataloged the hardcover as follows:
Names: Biespiel, David, 1964– author.
Title: The education of a young poet / David Biespiel.
Description: Berkeley, CA : Counterpoint Press, 2017.
Identifiers: LCCN 2017026011 | ISBN
    9781619029934
Subjects: LCSH: Biespiel, David, 1964– | Poets,
    American—20th century—Biography. | Creation
    (Literary, artistic, etc.) | Authorship.
Classification: LCC PS3552.I374 Z46 2017 | DDC
    811/.54 [B]—dc23
LC record available at https://lccn.loc.gov/2017026011

Paperback ISBN: 978-1-64009-110-8

*Cover design by Bill Smith*
*Book design by Fritz Metsch*

COUNTERPOINT
2560 Ninth Street, Suite 318
Berkeley, CA 94710
www.counterpointpress.com

Printed in the United States of America
Distributed by Publishers Group West

1  3  5  7  9  10  8  6  4  2

*For Brian Spears*

I assumed that everything would lead to complete failure, but I decided that didn't matter—that would be my life.

—JASPER JOHNS

# CONTENTS

# CONTENTS

# THE
# EDUCATION
# OF A
# YOUNG
# POET

# ELMA

My life in poetry began when Harry Borg left Ukraine for America in 1910.

*Life* is not the exact word. Since Harry was born in Cherniostrov in the Pale of Settlement in 1879, and I was born in Oklahoma in 1964. Between us is his eldest son and that son's eldest daughter and that daughter's youngest son, me.

Harry and me left Cherniostrov by train for Lviv—he was going on ahead of his wife and their two small sons. From Lviv we found passage to the States. Then we went by train again to Iowa. We were looking for a place we could afford. There was a young fellow near Elma, 160 miles north of Des Moines, who offered us something. Later there was a cart and a mule and then peddling rags and pots, second-hand coats and slacks and blouses, every day except Friday nights when, even if on the road and miles from Elma, Harry would take shelter overnight in a customer's barn to make Shabbat.

Riding the trains across the heartland was really in

vogue in those days. The cornfields were like a green ocean with shoals and shallows and waves. You could see humpback whales in the wind through the stalks, whales shivering in the underside of the midwestern air. Then suddenly, like a lighthouse, there'd be a silo. The wind was soft as flannel, too. The oaks longed for the sparrows and the sparrows longed for the sky and the sky longed for a wife. Days of rain blushing with passion and a quivery blessing. Me and Harry would stare and stare, smearing our eyes against the windows of the train. We were travelers who noticed every sun-weathered brick in the towns.

That summer the Iowa rivers receded under the trestles from the spring floods that had blossomed in July. The headstones in the cemeteries long ago had taken to peeling. At night the moon bristled over the open porches with the wicker chairs empty of their celibate lovers. The crossroads were like sideburns turned to gravel. We tumbled along the tracks, a little stoic, a little proud, a couple of puzzles needing to be solved. The dappled rows of shaggy corn sloping toward us plunged back into the velvet, green, windy distances. The rattle of the train faded again and again to the muffle of our sleep.

This was a time when polio was raging. There were 186 cases in Iowa that year. This was the summer of Halley's comet, too. Me and Harry could see it all right even from the train. It was no apparition. It was a match struck against eternity, an eyeless orphan. In 1986 I would look for Halley's comet again. I was living in the haze of cheap weed in Boston on Glenville Ave. near the expressionistic trees of Ringer Park. In Elma, though . . . Harry found Elma to have the kind of personality that was its own avant-garde. You couldn't erase Elma. Year after year the population decreased. But still the town remained. In 1910 Elma was eight hundred people and about to be re-designed with an orthodox Jew. Back then Elma was a town of aching look-alikes. There was the aroma of wood burn and laundry on the line. White farmhouses and neat fences. It was a place you could live in all your life but if you're weren't born there you were always an outsider. Every stranger could be a murderer. Harry arrived like new foliage.

I don't know the first thing about Elma really. The house me and Harry found had no broom and no locks, and the old siding clung to the building like a child to his mother's leg. We were like a work of art, Harry and me. When we were naked, you'd have thought the bottom of us was trying to escape the top. Our legs were deliberate, pointed, meager. Our chest was stout as a fire hydrant. It was tough to make us smile. This was so long ago. I can see one small room, that's it. It was a room where you could hear voices but no one was there. There was a chair and table and a rug. The silence of Iowa could fill that room from floor to ceiling, every hour. The silence was an unmentionable smudge. Only the habit of Harry's voice talking Yiddish would deflate the room's quiet. And the distant bark of dogs.

This room became the walls of every stanza I've ever known.

Harry talked to himself in those days in phrases like little sketches of poetry, without dropping his chin into his hands in contemplation. He'd assemble each syllable into a chant, an intonation. He'd talk to himself in the kitchen at morning and on his mattress at night. He'd talk to himself in the stairwell and on the way back from the market. He'd talk to himself while standing alone in the room, I remember that. What a time in America, he would say to himself. No war beginning or ending. Look at these simple pleasures of light and wind and stars, he'd say. What could be more attractive than Elma, Iowa, he'd ask, that God in his wisdom saw to building it up around the new train depot. He'd want to smile but it was a smile of cheap rent and cheap joy. There was dirt all right in 1910. Reams of it. What is dirt but life, he'd say.

Once I asked Harry why, or maybe it was how could you leave your wife, Rose, and your sons, Joseph and Irving, for America, and how long are you willing to wait to reunite? He turned to talk to the bathroom mirror then about the encryptions in his face that revealed nothing about how it was all going to turn out. Was your marriage, I asked, happy or unhappy? Were there disappointments? Let's not talk of dreams, he said, but of life in broad daylight. Let's talk of being a father but without sons in the house to listen. About duty. About right and wrong. Unruffled faith and limitless God.

There was so much praying alongside the talking, too, about the forgotten and the damned and the swollen heart. All this talking to himself Harry did in a language no one understood. This was the first pure poetry I ever knew. Sung out loud more or less to no one on a theme of longing. Wife. Sons. Rags for clothes. Snow. Stalks of corn. The unrepeatable finitude of sex and mute caresses of the mind. And of the *Sh'ma* spoken to the Iowa dust. "Hear, O, Israel, the Lord our God, the Lord is One"— spoken to the Iowa birds pecking on the ground.

For ten years he talked and prayed to himself, talked and prayed to the empty rooms.

Prayer was his beauty-utterance. He prayed about the lessons life could teach and about going along for the ride. He prayed about being wrong and feeling alive and then feeling lucky. When he heard the flies sing to him, he prayed about how easy life had become. When he heard the rain on the roof, he prayed about how hard life had become. He prayed about envy and jealousy and corruption and success. He prayed about the endlessness of truth and the endlessness of lies. Those Friday nights miles from home, cloudy or sunny or snowy or in blistering heat, there was Harry making Shabbat alone but for the rats in a customer's hay barn, where he would quietly rest in the presence of God, opening his soul as a man does, concerned only with the moments of time and his momentary sharing of the eternal. The hay bales would go dark as the night left him powerless to the forces of circumstance. Next day he'd gather his belongings into his rag cart and return alone to Elma.

Even in sleep he had dreams in the form of prayers about nerves and worries over money. There were prayers about gathering stones and breaking stones, about towns with no houses but a sheriff returning alone. One of his dream-prayers he had again and again was a rabbi telling him, "Look, young fellow, I'm going to tell you a few things about your reputation." But then he never did. The dream-prayers would fade and return. He'd awake weary and resigned. And resume his talking. He talked to himself every waking minute he was alone, talked to himself alone for ten years like that, talked to himself and talked to me in something resembling poems no one can remember—before at last by train in the winter of 1920 with a flowering white snow falling, a snow falling like stars filling the air, his wife Rose and sons Joseph, now thirteen, and Irving, now ten, arrive at the depot in Elma with a featherbed and two silver candlesticks. The older one had the sharp eyes of a boxer; the younger was tender, his hands like the soft leather on a baseball.

And Harry says to me, now my poetry belongs to America.

The first night Joseph Borg spent in Elma, Iowa, he woke up before dawn because he had to pee. He shook his silent father awake. For a moment he stared into the face of that strange man who he had not seen in ten years. Joseph didn't know a lick of English—he stared at his father's face the way a poet stares at a blank piece of paper where mostly the soul is at stake. He stared at the face like diving underwater against all odds of survival and finding there coincidences and afterthoughts, confessions of the weak who have little to say, finding smells and sounds and the passions of the body.

Pee in the snow, Harry said.

From the eaves of the house I could see thirteen-year-old Joseph tiptoe out the front door and lean over the edge of the porch—

*I attach tags, carve initials, pee on fireplugs*
*outlining my territory*

—so says Philip Whalen about peeing outside the dorms at Reed College thirty years later when he is the roommate of my cousin, Moshe, who is a first cousin of Ruth—who, in 1935, fifteen years after that night on the Iowa porch, would elope with Joseph in Chicago and become his wife. That night, watching Joseph's limber body above the snow, seeing his strong-willed teenage face with its sharp nose like something out of a folktale, I understand I could never take a dispassionate view of memory.

Perhaps the hardest thing about my education as a poet is watching the past reverse itself. It's like undressing. First you remove the jacket, then the shirt, the undershirt, and then you stand bare-chested in the cold air.

Then you step out of the trousers but no underwear or socks. Memory torments you like that. And when memory looks down the street of a small Christian town in America before dawn with the eyes of a thirteen-year-old Jewish boy who is standing half-dressed on the porch, and the stars grin at the secrets of the world, memory zips up its pants against the wind and carries on.

Then Joseph slipped. He was turning to go back into the house and lost his footing and nearly collapsed on the wood porch before he caught hold of the frozen railing. He hadn't meant to be in a rush. The cold air was pleasurable against his bare skin. But he understood that the earth and everything around him was so different now. Even his gait seemed messed up. Hurrying into the dark house with its fantasia of squat rooms, he began to float instead of walk. He floated backward and stretched his neck to see his way. He floated as in a painting by Chagall into the small kitchen above the countertops and sink and didn't stop to think about how strange it was to be in the air. A little blood was coming out of his hand where he'd cut it catching his fall. But he didn't find that strange either. Being hurt was the same as being humorous, he knew that already, same as being fatherless. Or nearly fatherless, he reminded himself, as he floated now down the hallway past his sleeping father and mother, his hair touching the ceiling, his arms sprawled. He began to float even lighter now, his fingers loose and the night air swelling around his body. He could see the footprints in the floors where his father had been walking for ten years. Those footprints and the frightening sounds they had made came up the stairs, padded through the halls, stumbled and straightened up. Joseph floated, powdery and white, bobbing up and down, his heart undestroyed. He wanted to babble and sing but instead smiled. And then he floated over to the narrow bed he was sharing with his little brother. Not falling into it but arriving as at the end of a triumph.

Joseph would always remember this night as a kind of improvised awakening. He would think of it when he had nothing else on his mind, the way one thinks of sex, always believing that it clarifies things for him, that he could understand other people through the filter of the night he flew in the house in Elma. Sometimes he saw it as a dream or as a memory. Other times he heard it as a song, a prayer. He'd be flying monotonously and then there'd be a variation—he'd sprout wings! he'd become an angel!—and then he'd hear the melody again. He could hear the song building and building in him, mounting and then descending, collapsing as he collapsed into bed.

Other times the memory was a question-and-answer routine. He would ask about simultaneity and answer about despair. He would ask about sadness and answer with proverbs. The questions and the answers synced up into a kind of rhythm about snow and sleep, birth and pain, but now in a language neither of us understood back then. This new English would sound like a chime to Joseph, a loud chime in a silent house. The chiming had a clear beat that sounded like, "Why should things be easy to understand?" It had a rhythm that meant, "Not every puzzle is intended to be solved." Joseph would hum and hum the passages of the chiming labyrinths of syllables. Once he reached the end, he would turn that into the beginning. He could hear the locks of words unlock like a truth to be grappled with. He would go on hearing the chime and the patterns they made in the mind, his and mine, and—on his knees, straining his neck—he would try to work them out into his new words but they didn't always match the design. He'd try to connect the points of sound.

From that, I discovered, a writer will find his own voice in the distortions and discolorations of the mouth.

# PEDAGOGY OF
# THE OPPRESSED

aking advantage of a diving scholarship, which paid my tuition, I enrolled at Boston University in 1982. I was in a hurry to leave Texas. Ever since I'd worked on Ted Kennedy's 1980 campaign in southwest Houston, which was a bitter loss to Jimmy Carter, I was restless with Texas and the conservative direction the state was taking. I felt a fast-fading interest in Judaism too and the Jewish neighborhood I'd grown up in, Meyerland. Most of my friends were headed to the University of Texas, where they would pledge the Jewish fraternities or sororities. Going to school in Boston was part of my new romance with liberalism even if my first night there I found myself—dressed in cowboy boots and a Stetson—standing in a humid autumn dusk in front of T's Pub at Comm. Ave. and Babcock Street when a cabbie cruised past, rolled down the window, and shouted, Fuck you, homeboy.

Boston became the wreck I wanted to dive into. It became—

*the wreck and not the story of the wreck*
*the thing itself and not the myth*

I didn't know those lines from Adrienne Rich's poem then, but I knew that Boston was as good as it was going to get for me. It was a map out of the damage of my self-awareness and into some new evidence of beauty. Boston was my future, and Adrienne Rich's ideas about making new myths were waiting even for someone like me, a homeboy from Harris County.

Like the city itself, the university was not at its best when I arrived in 1982. People went to BU to party. The people in the student union were dressed for keggers. They expected a party every night. In the student union I recognized the Jewish kids instantly, and there were a lot of them. The boys were nattier cousins of the kids I'd grown up with at the synagogue. The girls were going in for the Cyndi Lauper look. We all struck poses, but there wasn't a lot of self-examination to go with it. It was like I'd left home two thousand miles away and arrived in my Hebrew School cafeteria. The bohemians were somewhere, but I hadn't found them yet.

Feeling alien within the familiar became one of the first stances I undertook when I began to write poems. Boston taught me that. It taught that strangeness was no more odd than a bird's foot. I hadn't left Texas entirely, I soon discovered. BU's president, John Silber, a Kantian, was from San Antonio. Silber was the kind of man who couldn't bring himself to flatter even the shyest freshman. By the time I arrived on campus, President Silber was at war with the faculty over unionization and the campus's South African divestment movement. Silber's public enemy at BU was historian Howard Zinn. I was but a lowly foot soldier in the undergraduate army of Howard Zinn's political causes, but I believed fully in his general notion that there is no higher form of patriotism than dissent. A lot of days we'd be demonstrating in Marsh Plaza, and no matter the cause, whether it was against the Pentagon or apartheid or the BU cops, against the Reagan administration, the Silber administration, or against obedience generally—"historically, the most terrible things (war, genocide, and slavery) have occurred not from disobedience, but from obedience," Zinn shouted into a bullhorn during one lunchtime demonstration—we were rallying in order to tell a new story about ourselves, how we valued ourselves, and our futures. I wasn't writing poems yet, but that ideal spurred my interest in the possibility of poetry when I first started to write a few years later.

All the courses I took then were about how small actions for good, if accomplished by millions and millions of people and performed one person and one action at a time, amounted to the most transformative change the world could ever know. The change could affect government, families, love, work. Our democracy—and this we believed almost blindly—was imperiled. Our loves, our work, our perceptions of time and history, our aesthetics—all of it was wrong. Change had to come. The country could corporatize and militarize the liberal arts, but individual learning must remain radical because the individual must resist power and be invested in the future.

The professors, even in the English department, were like revolutionaries who extolled protest generally as the pinnacle of human dignity. In a dozen accents, they taught us that literature was the art that showed us that human beings should live in defiance of power, and that to live fully and gloriously in a succession of present moments would be to triumph over injustice. A lot of students barely understood what was being said to them.

I took a course in education, given by Henry Giroux. Tuesday and Thursday mornings he paced at the bottom of the sloping auditorium in the School of Education. With long black hair he reminded me of the pop star Rick Springfield who made it big with "Jessie's Girl" the year before. I was spellbound by his lectures. I remember the morning he told us life was a war zone and that government, in the form of public schools, were predators against the citizenry, against the poor and minorities and immigrants, and especially against defenseless children. Giroux told us we needed to combine all critical theory with social action. He seemed to despise us, that's for sure, and made it clear he thought most public school teachers were hostile to individual freedom and social reconstruction. Many students were vocally opposed to his ideology. But I accepted everything he said. I took Giroux's side in the classroom debates as naturally as I took to breathing.

He didn't know it then, none of us did, but Giroux was about to be denied tenure by President Silber even though he'd received a unanimous vote at all levels of his academic review and was one of only three cases up for tenure that year that were unanimous. Giroux's dean declared that he would resign if Giroux didn't get tenure, but Silber denied it—not before first offering Giroux a second chance if he agreed not to publish anything for two years and to study logic and science personally with Silber.

I learned about Paulo Freire from Giroux and dog-eared the hell out of Freire's book, *Pedagogy of the Oppressed*. When Freire—who taught language to non-native speakers by Scotch-taping onto every object in their home the word in the new language that corresponds with that object so that they could learn a new language from their lived experience and not through a textbook—wrote that it is "not the helpless, subject to terror, who initiate terror, but the violent, who with their power create the concrete situation which begets the 'rejects of life . . . ,' not the tyrannized who initiate despotism, but the tyrants . . . not those whose humanity is denied them who negate humankind, but those who denied that humanity (thus negating their own as well) . . . [and that] Force is used not by those who have become weak under the preponderance of the strong, but by the strong who have emasculated them," I fully understood that language can never be neutral.

One morning after Giroux's class, while I was sitting on a bench in the lobby of the School of Education, a tall student with a mop of brown hair and a dark mustache was walking directly toward me with a page-boy blonde at his side. He asked if we could talk. Sure, I said. In class that morning I'd been arguing with the notion that all education comes about through the process of living, so I wondered whether the two of them were from the education-just-to-secure-a-job side of the debate. He was enormously tall, six foot ten, I thought, six foot eleven maybe, maybe seven feet tall. At my diminished height, I figured it would be more strategic if I remained seated. I ceremoniously crossed my legs. I want to be *your* friend, he said, declaring, I'm Giff, then introducing me to the girl. Relieved, I said hello, and we talked some of our affection for Giroux. Then the three of us wandered out to the Charles River to kill time. Sitting down on the cool October grass, Giff pulled out a joint and lit it.

With that, we blew off the rest of the day. The girl by then had left for work, and the orange and gold leaves were blowing back toward Comm. Ave. From its source just north of Echo Lake in Hopkinton, Massachusetts, the Charles passed through two dozen towns until it reached us at its mouth along the campus of BU to form the border between Boston and Cambridge. In that moment as we sat in the grass near the campus and later walked along the brown river in the day's fine blue light, all things were merging together. The city was cut by the river and was running alongside us as if from the beginning of creation. Under the Charles River was a haunting I struggled to hear. I wanted the knowledge to flow from me like the river flowed. And I wanted time to flow, too. I could feel how even from its far-off source all the way to the Atlantic, the river was in all places at once. We watched the river glow and quicken. We talked about how the river could wash away all love and all pain and go on existing without any obligation. We didn't know it then but we were on our way to becoming lifelong friends. We did know that the river was opening up to us like a book to be read. The swift current was at first baffling, but then we understood its anguish for freedom.

I had been attending Robert Levine's modern poetry class, where we had read Walt Whitman in the slender blue *Norton Anthology*, and while walking back to Giff's apartment in Allston later that afternoon I read a favorite passage from the opening of "Song of Myself" about a blade of grass:

> *I guess it must be the flag of my disposition, out of*
> *hopeful green stuff woven.*
>
> *Or I guess it is the handkerchief of the Lord,*
> *A scented gift and remembrancer designedly*
> *dropped,*

*Bearing the owner's name someway in the corners,*
  *that we may see and remark, and say Whose?*

*Or I guess the grass is itself a child . . . the produced*
  *babe of the vegetation.*

*Or I guess it is a uniform hieroglyphic,*
*And it means, Sprouting alike in broad zones and*
  *narrow zones,*
*Growing among black folks as among white*
*Kanuck, Tuckahoe, Congressman, Cuff, I give them*
  *the same, I receive them the same.*

*And now it seems to me the beautiful uncut hair of*
  *graves.*

*Tenderly will I use you curling grass,*
*It may be you transpire from the breasts of young*
  *men,*
*It may be if I had known them I would have loved*
  *them;*
*It may be you are from old people and from women,*
  *and from offspring taken soon out of their*
  *mother's laps,*
*And here you are the mother's laps.*

*This grass is very dark to be from the white heads of*
  *old mothers,*

*Darker than the colorless beards of old men,*
*Dark to come from under the faint red roofs of mouths.*

*O I perceive after all so many uttering tongues!*
*And I perceive they do not come from the roofs of*
    *mouths*
*for nothing.*

*I wish I could translate the hints about the dead*
    *young men and women,*
*And the hints about old men and mothers, and the*
    *offspring taken soon out of their laps.*

We had stopped at the curve where Comm. Ave. split off
from Brighton Ave. Let me read something, Giff said,
taking the book in his hands. Read these lines, I said,
number eleven. He affected a theatrical intonation:

*The beards of the young men glisten'd with wet, it*
    *ran from their long hair,*
*Little streams pass'd all over their bodies.*

*An unseen hand also pass'd over their bodies,*
*It descended tremblingly from their temples and ribs.*

*The young men float on their backs, their white*
    *bellies bulge to the sun, they do not ask who*
    *seizes fast to them,*

*They do not know who puffs and declines with*
    *pendant and bending arch,*
*They do not think whom they souse with spray.*

The high point of Levine's class was his discussion of Whitman's "When I Heard the Learn'd Astronomer." I read it to Giff as we came out of Brookline Liquor with a six-pack of beer and some wine from the two-for-five-dollar bin:

*When I heard the learn'd astronomer,*
*When the proofs, the figures, were ranged in*
    *columns before me,*
*When I was shown the charts and diagrams, to*
    *add, divide, and measure them,*
*When I sitting heard the astronomer where he*
    *lectured with much applause in the lecture-room,*
*How soon unaccountable I became tired and sick,*
*Till rising and gliding out I wander'd off by myself,*
*In the mystical moist night-air, and from time to*
    *time,*
*Look'd up in perfect silence at the stars.*

A lot of the students had read the poem as a rejection of acquired knowledge in favor of direct experience. But I saw it, even then, as the combination of acquired knowledge and direct experience that is topped off by honest and imaginative interpretation. One leads you to the other.

Study leads to experience, and experience leads to study. Imagination leads to forms, and forms lead to knowledge of the past. Speaking leads to listening which leads to silence and a fresh entrance into a new understanding of existence. And then the poem that follows revivifies the experience and offers a journey into a fresh insight.

The first poetry reading I went to was at Blacksmith House in Cambridge. The poet was William Matthews. I don't remember much of the reading. Matthews was funny, I remember, especially his badinage, and everyone there seemed to know him personally except me. I do remember what happened afterward. It was April 14, 1986, and the United States was bombing Libya. I'd stopped in a loud bar in Cambridge on the way back to Allston and could see General Colin Powell defending the American air strikes as a response to the bombing of a discotheque in Berlin. The second poetry reading I went to was at MIT. I had gone to meet a girl from Minnesota I knew from Pat Craddock's literary studies seminar. Gail Whitney was an editor of *Ex Libris*, BU's student literary journal. She had a crooked smile and straight, dark hair that was wonderfully askew in the mornings we woke up together. She was like a river herself those mornings, leisurely rolling over and mild, listening (I believed) to my heart rushing with blood. The poet that night at MIT was Robert Creeley, but I didn't know his poems then. Whitney showed up on the arm of another boy, as well. Later I learned he was a new boyfriend, or an old boyfriend, it's hard to remember. Neither of us were expecting drama. The lecture hall was enormously crowded, and we tried not to look at each other. Creeley kept interrupting his reading with nostalgic stories from his youth in the 1940s like the night he went skinny dipping in the Charles River while he was an undergraduate at Harvard. Then he'd read another one of his miniatures, something like "A Night Sky"—

*All the grass*
*dies*
*in front of us.*

*The fire*
*again*
*flares out.*

*The night*
*such a large*
*place. Stars*

*the points,*
*but like*
*places no*

*depth, I see*
*a flat—*
*a plain as if the*

*desert*
*were showing smaller*
*places.*

Later on that day I met Giff, back at his apartment on Royce Road, a woman dressed in a sleeveless Anarkali suit was high, and she was dancing to the new Dylan album, *Infidels*. Giff was dancing alongside her. She seemed to be blissfully vacating her body as if tomorrow was never going to arrive. But then she turned on Giff—who now seemed to me more like six foot six and not seven feet after all, dressed in torn jeans, a blue Grateful Dead T-shirt, and barefoot, and all the while holding a spent roach between his thumb and forefinger—and she says, I wish I had a cock like you guys. You can have mine, Giff said in return and took one of her hands. The music kept playing. The song was "Sweetheart Like You"—

> *You know, I once knew a woman who looked like you*
> *She wanted a whole man, not just a half*
> *She used to call me sweet daddy when I was only a*
> *    child*
> *You kind of remind me of her when you laugh*
> *In order to deal in this game, got to make the queen*
> *    disappear*
> *It's done with a flick of the wrist*
> *What's a sweetheart like you doing in a dump like*
> *    this?*

She seemed not to have heard him because her face betrayed nothing back. Then, she raised her arms toward the ceiling as if she wanted to take flight, but instead collapsed onto the floor and began to wail like a cat along to the music. She howled, give me my own cock, give me mine.

I was sitting in an armchair in the corner of the living room watching them dance. I thought about who this girl might have been and where she came from and how had they met and what might have been going on inside her head. Giff had turned his attention to the next song, the sarcastic anthem "Neighborhood Bully," and motioned me to listen. Listening was something I was trying hard to get better at. I wanted to hear the ways language could touch itself and be a small act of kindness or a clarity for living. I wanted to hear how that sort of power could turn a life around. I was trying to listen to the high and low notes of people's voices and the messages that those tones conveyed. Like Walt Whitman in "Song of Myself," I wanted to accrue what I heard from the political and the poetic deep into my body. Giff was standing at the window now after putting the needle back at the beginning of "Neighborhood Bully." He was mouthing the words in my direction so I could see him singing—

*Well, the neighborhood bully, he's just one man*
*His enemies say he's on their land*

*They got him outnumbered about a million to one*
*He got no place to escape to, no place to run*

Listen! He was calling to me, and then pointing to the
turntable, calling to the girl, listen to this cock!—

*The neighborhood bully been driven out of every*
*    land*
*He's wandered the earth an exiled man*
*Seen his family scattered, his people hounded and*
*    torn*
*He's always on trial for just being born*

The two of them were dancing again. I was rolling another joint poorly with the shake tapering out of the
ends. I had never felt farther away from Texas at that
moment nor more at home. Giff was looking right at me.
He was shouting, Dylan's back!

All of it—the dancing, the new friendship, the music,
Walt Whitman, the Charles River—was becoming in
my light hallucination a casual orchestra with an untold
number of instruments and repertoire. The streetlights
were on now and seemed to gaze into the window of the
apartment like the eyes of God that wanted all of us in
there to undress. I could hear my imagination and the
ragged metaphors swimming in the mud in my head.

# PRETENDING NOT
# TO PRETEND

I hadn't been living on Glenville Ave. with Giff, Nick, and Paul very long when a girl who'd recently graduated from Boston University in physics—and with whom, clandestinely, I'd been prowling around, and I'd been having vague imaginings of what it would be like to steal her away from her new husband, a jazz student who went to Berklee—slipped into our apartment one night and sat down on my bed. She removed her blouse and bra and skirt and climbed under the covers next to me. She simply explained that her husband was not the right person for her, and that I was.

Her breath smelled of cigarettes and sambuca, and her exposition was tender. I didn't understand at first what she was talking about. She hardly referred to the submerged emotions between us as real, and my impression was that she was describing two people who existed in a dream. When I was fully awake and understood what was happening, I was trying to imagine quickly how this might now go. She had already wrapped one of her legs over mine and was resting her head on my shoulder. We kissed a little between trying to get comfortable or situated or something, moving our hands all over, into each others' thighs and curves, the length of a shoulder, all of our stifled silence fading into our feet. And then with her head resting for a minute on my chest, she drifted to sleep. This was no way for a romance to start. Yet what she said seemed already to be dissipating out the window into the damp air.

She had talked other times about her relationship to her husband as if she were talking about the relationship between motion and mechanics. She was eccentric that way. She was the kind of girl who was all about forces that needed to act upon an object to get it moving. She'd met her husband while they both attended a private school in Vienna or Paris, I was never sure. They moved to Boston and took classes, and against her parents' wishes got married. Giff and I had gone to the after-party at their apartment on Summit Ave. Her mother had agreed to attend, but she sat alone, wearing a frown, while the wedding partiers smoked hashish and drank cheap wine around her and listened to albums by Abdullah Ibrahim. The cigarette and hash smoke was, I thought, intended as a healing ritual for us all. We became suspended and unfolded and iridescent. Several people collapsed from the euphoria onto the floor. The entire room was tingling with the aura of inhaling and drinking and inaction.

The bride asked me to bring a poem, and so I read Dickinson's #917—

*Love – is anterior to Life –*
*Posterior – to Death –*
*Initial of Creation, and*
*The Exponent of Earth –*

There was a lot of nodding of heads after I sat down. The bride's mother asked for a copy, and I remember feeling deeply moved by this and was glad to give it to her. I hadn't experienced then how poetry could matter to anyone who wasn't young. Did you write this, the mother asked. I was wondering if the smoke from the hashish and cigarettes was getting to her. No, I said, nobody alive could write that.

During the weeks after the wedding the husband seemed little interested in his new wife, at least compared to his guitar. She was easily bored, too, and fell into reading English novels, and we talked about books in my apartment or while wandering around Ringer Park on Allston Street. She had a thing for Tess from Hardy's *Tess of the d'Urbervilles*. She described Tess in terms of physics, that Tess understood motion, and that the forces of the energy in her life were weighed against her. Around the time she slipped into my apartment she was teaching physics in Walpole at the high school and had created a minor scandal by letting her students take poppers in her classroom—Popics, the *Boston Phoenix* had reported when the scandal broke, was what they called her physics class.

In the morning she was in a rush to catch the T and get to school. She had told me she had been standing under my window for an hour and was hoping I'd just suddenly come walking up the street, by and by, or be heading out of the apartment. Then she decided to let herself in. At first, she said, she just stood in the foyer as if still waiting for an invitation. She said she and her husband were disinterested in each other. She needed someone who was less like her.

We were in the narrow hallway now. I was leaning up against the wall, and the other guys were walking by us, semi-casually going through their morning routines, excusing themselves but eyeing the melodrama that was opening our day, shooting quick, inquisitive glances into my line of sight. She said she had been reading Derrida so much lately. Using words like *pretending to pretend*, she said she can only love in one language but not her own. She was completely still, her head down, her straight dark hair pulled into a ponytail, and standing in the center of the little hall. She kept trying to light a cigarette and wouldn't let me do it for her. Her voice was spinning silk. I listened to it, first intently, and then with less fascination, feeling she was going to say what she was going to say.

I have conviction, she was saying, I'm not strange or threatening. She went on, building up the mechanics of her argument that began, earlier in bed, to be about us, and became, in the hallway, about her and her husband. She was suddenly turning into a deconstructionist orator on love, and I couldn't get what she was saying unmixed up from what she was referencing about Derrida. It might as well have been something like, "Love is only possible when one of the warring sides takes the first step. The future of love, the future, *l'avenir,* must arrive unexpectedly. We can't have that now." She was pulling her handbag over her shoulder to leave the apartment, and I felt I understood she needed me to release her and I just said, it's okay. Then I thought, as a matter of valor, to match her Derrida for Derrida. I said, you and I must be given over to absolute solitude, and no one can speak for us. We must take love upon ourselves, each of us must do that. Or something like that. I was just trying to let her leave. Derrida meant little to me. Questions of duplication, duplicity, and iterability left me cold next to things like waking up at night with a seductive woman slipping unannounced into my bed. But not that, not that exactly. I was trying to understand how words and images and silences offered me meaning out of themselves, earnestly and tangibly, like a dream of a universe I might hold or fashion in my mind and hands. And, although I wasn't writing poems yet, I was beginning to wonder about becoming a writer and how writing helps to change the shape of the universe. Might I be a witness to those impulses? Just then she walked out of the apartment, caught up in her deconstructionist vindication, panting and smiling to herself on the way down the stairs. In the silence that followed, I didn't feel any anger, just amusement. I went back to my room, made the bed, and got dressed. I had a date to meet Whitney, the girl I'd avoided at the Creeley reading a few nights back, for breakfast.

When you diagnose your life in relation to what it teaches you about becoming a writer, the thing that surprises you is how your original sources take place long before you're even alive. It's easy to forget this. We might perceive life coming to us in patterns or in random bursts. And, as writers, we share moments. Just as a body, like water, retains no constant shape, so in memory there are no constant conditions.

As I say, the thing that surprises you is how your original sources take place long before you're even alive. When my grandfather Joseph Borg left Elma, Iowa, for college at the University of Minnesota in the late 1920s, his English was still so rough he struggled to pass his classes and could only afford to attend one semester besides. But once there he did meet Ruth Lenske. He was going by Joe then, and something of their courtship and elopement remains a mystery to me. The writer in me knows I was with Joe Borg all that time, same as I was with Harry Borg when he came to America two decades earlier. To think otherwise would be to lose some literary capacity or to believe that the imagination doesn't exist.

Believing I can see Joe come to Ruth's parents' house on Upton Avenue North a couple of weeks after they meet is to see the sloping sidewalk and the low windows alight in the sun. Looking at Joe, who was now stocky and dark and handsome in his twenties, and whose sharp nose and lean face and dark eyes were beautiful, is to see a younger but also older version of myself. When Joe spoke to Ruth in a soft Yiddish accent that had little English fluency as they walked in her neighborhood, I could hear thousands of years of phantasms in his syllables. Yet here we were, me and Joe—a poor freshmen from Iowa, a son of an immigrant rag peddler—invading Minneapolis, and trying to walk and talk like a gentleman.

In love, Joe felt his sense of decorum deepen. And what was she thinking, we wondered? Had she seen Joe's politeness as exquisitely assured or as arrogance? She loved to read, and I could feel her look at us as if we were a book full of a book's purities and failings. She had bookish eyes that, like sleep, appeared to touch eternity—an eternity that carried with it overtures of wind and birds that invent the horizon by their flight and the unsolvable puzzle of rain. She was born in Minneapolis. But Joe was born in Ukraine, so she seemed to see in us a story of endurance. She wanted that story. But not everything was written yet. She would walk the university corridors with Joe on the way to her job at the campus laundry and search his eyes like shelves in a library and rearrange his meanings and coherences, his inspirations and failures and cacophonies, his past and his future, his thoughts even, and she could feel how fond he was of her, how the symmetry between them moved them both like a voice telling a great story. Everything he said to her came right out of his own journey to America. When he told her about stealing onto the train with his mother and small brother in Cherniostrov, she was spellbound—

You taste books like food, Ruth, but I believe in action, in doing. We were supposed to leave Cherniostrov and rejoin my dad in 1914 but the war came. I was seven then. And then we had papers to leave in 1917 but the Revolution came, and all that meant nothing when the Bolsheviks passed through the town—

He didn't ramble or get confused or repeat himself, but was emotionally assured, even if bits and pieces of his English slipped into Yiddish—

Then one night mother says we're going, and she takes me and Irving and we hop onto a boxcar headed to Lviv. In the boxcar are some soldiers and—what do you call—*shlepers*, and some of them knew us from the town. Next day the train is stopped by a couple of Cossacks. They try to take my mother and us from the train, but one of the soldiers in the boxcar protected us. He knew my mother. She was his bootlegger. That's right. She was his bootlegger. She sold liquor for money after my father left for America—

In telling the story of one's coming into consciousness, all languages are more or less the same. The words for mud and train-carriage and urine and dirt and bare feet are different, but the ascendency from a valley to a peak is the same. Yiddish, for Joe, like sex, was where the moral drama of his mind was. That's what I was thinking anyway as I listened to him tell his story to Ruth. When he looked at Ruth, he kept looking at the way her fingers dangled from her hands, and his eyes would rest on the middle of her face as if he were trying to read her reflections. She would shudder listening to him talk. To Joe and me, she would appear afflicted—that's the word really, *afflicted*—with how his story kept him alive. It was like listening to a good piece of music, her eyes seemed to say, and she would cry as she listened to his song. Joe would look back at her in astonishment and get silent for a long time. He could hear that music too. It was slow, and he tried to listen hard to it. He hoped it wouldn't stop. Then she would listen again, too, with such intensity. She was undressed by his story and ready to be touched by it. How beautiful she was to him in those moments with the darkness between their bodies—and both of them being unable to move—and her face glistening. Your story is good for us, she kept saying, in a voice soft as a robe that he wished to draw away and re-move from her so her flesh appears and her hands lift to him, and the small acts of his words and her listening, and also his listening back to her words, unite. And her breath leaves her body. And her hands are moving up to his curly hair and over his sturdy shoulders.

The appeal of the body is hard to shake for a writer who, I will later discover, must write as if he has never been taught anything about love, and knows everything, as if he has never traveled anywhere but understands every step of the journey, every noun and verb of every language, and who has never given a second's thought about anything of importance but understands everything.

# OLD FRIENDS

Five or six months after moving to Boston, I got a job in an underground bookshop in Kenmore Square. The bookshop was next door to the Rathskeller, a gritty music joint everyone called the Rat. Inside the Rat was a jukebox, beer posters, a stage on crates for the bands, and picnic tables where you could eat barbecue from Hoodoos. Next to the Rat were nightclubs, pizza joints, a record store. There was a head shop, a packie, and a karate store too, along with junkies and homeless guys and hookers. This was a totally new work environment for me. When I was in high school in Houston I had worked in an upscale toy shop in the Galleria on Westheimer Road. It was a dull job in a swank shopping mall. Going to work at the Galleria felt like living on the set of a soap opera—something out of Port Charles or Oakdale—with so many patrons dressed up in slacks and ascots and alligator boots, or nylons and heels and clanky jewelry.

Some nights the toy store traffic would all but stop before we'd close up, and I could steal time reading out of a little poetry anthology I'd taken from my mother's library. It was Oscar Williams's *A Little Treasury of Modern Poetry: English and American* that had been published in the 1950s and probably my mother used it at the University of Michigan when she was an undergraduate there. Oscar Williams wasn't his real name though. His real name was Oscar Kaplan. In 1907, at the age of seven, Oscar Kaplan arrived to New York City with his parents from a Russian shtetl, Letychiv, which is only a hundred miles north of Cherniostrov where my great-grandparents had been born. Robert Frost was one of my favorite poets in the *Little Treasury* anthology, and I would memorize lines of his and then distort them under my breath for the right occasion. Asked to sweep the back room of the toy shop, I'd murmur, "Some say the world will end in fire. / Some say in ice. / But from what I've tasted of desire / Sweeping the back room is just as nice / And would suffice." For a while there I had "Directive" memorized. It was thrilling to think that poets were reinventing the world for us, and that I could drop in and out of that world whenever I wanted.

Until the era of buying a typewriter for everyday use came to an end, I would test out storeroom models by typing the first two sentences from Frost's "Birches"—

*When I see birches lean from left to right*
*Across the lines of straighter darker trees,*
*I like to think some boy's been swinging them.*
*But swinging doesn't bend them down to stay*
*As ice storms do.*

I liked thinking I was always in the market for a type-writer then. I preferred manuals and favored cast-iron Royals. The first word processor I ever typed on was a 1983 Apple Macintosh that a friend of mine at Boston University owned. Her boyfriend also sold pot, so there were additional inviting reasons to visit her group house on Boulevard Terrace in Allston. Before I took up rooms on Glenville Ave., I lived in that house with her and a reporter and her novelist boyfriend who'd just graduated from the Iowa Writers Workshop, and with various other BU transients.

Most of my work at the bookshop in Kenmore Square was loading and unloading boxes, stripping covers off mass-market paperbacks to return for credit from the publishers, and working the register weekend nights when the manager went home early. In his late twenties the manager wasn't much older than me. But to a college kid not yet twenty, he seemed wise beyond my imaginings. We called him Pete, but that wasn't his name. His girlfriend, who was the assistant manager, we called her Madame X. Everyone in the store had a nickname. Mine was the Kid. "Madame X," Pete would call out, "get the Kid to bring up the new shipment of books." Then I'd murmur, "bringing up the new shipment of books is just as nice / And would suffice."

Working in a bookshop nearly perfected the romance of myself as a liberal intellectual in Boston. The whole concept was enchanting, this combination of passion and the poetic. It was what riding the boxcars across the country must have been like. The 1980s had a lot of secondhand bookshops in Boston. I'd never known anything like them in Houston. Wandering into the Boston Book Annex on Beacon Street or the downtown Brattle Book Shop, or even cruising the shelves of some of the seedy basement bookshops in Brookline or Cambridge, long gone now and whose names escape me, was like entering the hidden rooms of secret relatives. Then to have those used books stacked up on the floor in your own bedroom back at your apartment, books that weren't assigned to you for courses but that you felt you had to have, was to display who your people were, your idealized family of intimates. It was to show your mind and heart to the world, and your mind and heart were bound up with yellowed pages and dried glue and old ink.

That's what Anatole Broyard says. He says, finding books is like "a reunion, like meeting old friends or lovers." Wandering Boston's used bookshops, strolling for hours like a pilgrim among the undisturbed dust, I would look for a life I had not yet known. Handling a

1937 Dell Book paperback edition of William Faulkner's *Mosquitoes* with its bodice-ripper cover and bright letters hailing the book as "A Brilliant Novel of Bohemian Life" was like picking the lock to a world of love teeming with artists and writers. The boatloads of bohemians in books like Faulkner's really owned the bookstores anyway rather than the other way around. They would run wild in the pages of novels and in my hands. All the blots and dog-ears made the books even more desirable. The scribbled notes in the margins were like traces of archeological bones, and you'd know that someone had read this one copy before and probably did so while sipping tea and waiting for the toast to pop up or the Red Sox game to come on the radio while outside through an opened window there'd be a humid Boston summer wind and aroma of green trees. These dim rooms of books were a sanctuary even if, and maybe because, thousands of pages in there remained untouched. The possibilities were eternal.

It wasn't that books were an escape from my own life or family, but they were a new manifestation and embodiment of my existence. Their archetypes and exemplars were palpable. I'd learned in Margaret Kennedy's high school Latin classes at Bellaire High School that this phenomenon was called *prosopopoeia* by the Latin and Greek writers. The term means more than just personification. The term means the speech of the imaginary. Literally, it means to make an eye or to make a face, a mask, through which—I would later think of it—a poet speaks. I realize that people implicitly understand this idea when reading books. But I took this concept to the level of love, I really did. This speaking mask was where a book began and ended for me. The masks were more than just the human variety. The settings and geographies and plots, the metaphors and stanzas, the clothing and histories and voices—all of it became something embodied. And then I became embodied by all of that, too. The books seemed to get inside my own blood. The words escaped into me. And then I would try to see or re-see—revise—the world with this new blood inside my body. It was like a drug, and only taking mushrooms and letting my brain get shagged with the glitter of hallucination where what is and isn't present can be held at once came close to the experience.

Sometimes I wasn't sure what I'd have done without books when I was an undergraduate. Think about sex, I guess, more. The distraction was shuddering. My earliest favorites came out of the blue *Norton Anthology of Modern Poetry*. Whitman, Dickinson, Hopkins, Yeats, Stevens, Lawrence, Owen, Bogan, Crane, Kavanaugh, Penn Warren, Kunitz, Auden, and Roethke dominated my reading of the early half of modern poetry in England and America. I'd studied Pound and Eliot and Williams in one of my courses but seldom brought them home. My reading instead was a kind of hysterical pleasure-seeking of what Yeats calls "what is past, or passing, or to come."

I had imagined myself like Doctor Dolittle studying, not animals, but books. And not books exactly but individual lines from individual poems. Lines and phrases—I was obsessed then with the magic of assonance and consonance. I was reading, not even the words exactly, but the physical letters of words. The English alphabet left me afire and itchy and wild-eyed. The letter *I*, I mean, it's just a single, straight scratch on the page. But the concepts we earnestly apply to that vertical bone—the self, individuality, the imagination, the mind, the sensual body—could topple a government.

My mother's mother held portions of *Beowulf* from memory, as well as the opening lines of *The Canterbury Tales* and passages of Shakespeare. My father's mother used to read to me when I was small, and like a lot of children I enjoyed touching the books as she read *The Gingerbread Man* or *Peter Rabbit*. Mother's library at home was a mix of political science, Jewish history (the red letters on the binding of *The Rise and Fall of the Third Reich* would shine down at you from the highest shelf like a spotlight from a guard tower), and a sprinkling of drama. She'd studied Ibsen in college and had a tender, heartbroken affection for *A Doll's House* and *Hedda Gabler*. My father had kept his childhood illustrated paperbacks of *Tarzan* and Agatha Christie mysteries and Sherlock Holmes, and these were available to me as boy, as were hand-me-down editions of Companion Library books. We had—

*The Adventures of Huckleberry Finn* | *The Adventures of Tom Sawyer*

*The Swiss Family Robinson* | *Robinson Crusoe*

*The Jungle Book* | *The Wizard of Oz*

*The Little Lame Prince* | *The Merry Adventures of Robin Hood*

*Just So Stories* | *The Prince and the Pauper*

*Little Men* | *Little Women*

*Gulliver's Travels* | *Treasure Island*

*A Dog of Flanders* | *Tom Sawyer Abroad*

*Kidnapped* | *Tom Sawyer, Detective*

*Andersen's Fairy Tales* | *Grimms' Fairy Tales*

*Heidi* | *Hans Brinker*

*Alice in Wonderland* and *Through the Looking-Glass* | *Five Little Peppers and How They Grew*

*Aesop's Fables* | *Arabian Nights*

And then there was the *siddur*, the Jewish prayer book, I held in my lap Friday nights or Saturday mornings at Congregation Beth Yeshurun on Beechnut Street in Houston. The rough, hardbound cover always felt like a rugged block of black stone from a destroyed cemetery—a stone that had been passed around, hand to hand, for thousands of years. Nothing in the *siddur* led me to radical amazement, not once, but the shapes of the Hebrew letters and the translations in English offered me a route into a pilgrimage of language that I gladly took. The wonder I was expected to express toward God I found myself showing toward words alone. While those around me were engaged in prayer and song and praise to God, I usually—especially as a teenager—was aware that the words were inviting me into something unutterable, into something beyond the limits of language. Abraham Joshua Heschel says, "In our own lives the voice of God speaks slowly, a syllable at a time." But I wasn't hearing the words as God's. Instead, I was hearing them as human creations. I was becoming awed by the wide horizon of the speech that arose out of an individual life lived in a single era and generation. Somewhere off in the horizon of the inner life of words, I felt, were things of common significance and complex meanings.

In the bookshop in Kenmore Square, especially late at night on the weekends when I usually worked, I took an interest in each of the customers who came in and wondered what particular motivation brought them into the shop at that hour. You could hear the rough music from the Rat blasting through the thin walls. I watched how the customers touched the books or kept their hands to their sides. I wondered what brought anyone to pull down *How to Win Friends and Influence People* from one aisle and Homer's *The Iliad* from the next. I wanted to understand what kind of people they were through the books they held and bought and took home. Sometimes customers would stand at the counter after paying at the cash register and talk about the books they were about to depart with, as if they were talking about a new child or pet. I had no trouble listening to them. On and on they came into the store, roaming the little aisles, choosing their little books, returning to the ordinariness of their lives. They were so like me, trading their daily lives for the new inner lives of words.

# AGAINST OUR WILL

My brothers took me to St. Luke's Hospital in Houston's medical district to see my father, who had collapsed earlier in the day with an aneurysm and stroke. This was March 1976. My brothers were still in high school, and I'd turned twelve a week earlier. My father was forty-six, and my mother, forty, was beside herself. I vaguely remember writing in a small diary I kept then something about the warm Texas winter air feeling "biblical," and that my father appeared in his hospital cot in the ICU "like a ghost of an orphan." A bit melodramatic, but if anyone noted that my father's stroke was too real for a novel much less a diary, I don't remember it. The suddenness of his illness had that kind of feeling anyway and, from that day on, my father never regained the full use of his speech. Words blew out of his mouth like ash.

The hospital was over on Holcombe Boulevard. Everyone knew the upper floors were reserved for the most critical patients. By the time we arrived in the late afternoon, visiting hours were over. I could just stand on tiptoe to look through the high window in the door into the intensive care ward. That's when I saw a part of him only, as if he were effaced. A hospital room is never just a single room. Implicit in its rectangular shapes are hundreds of thousands of other ones just like it all over the world. Everyone, from the patients to their concerned families, are in the hands of the hospital staff. There is always the odor—aroma, stench, redolence—of disinfectant and linoleum, and always the hum and whiff of lifeless air-conditioning and florescent lighting and bouquets of despair. Every view of the corners of hallways and shut windows and couches and the sound of ringing telephones, every glimpse of a sterile clipboard and all the discomforts, every parked wheelchair in the wide, white halls that might still hold the spirits of some lethargic stupor, invite you to reconstruct your life. What I could see in my father's corner of the ICU through the little square window at the top of the door wasn't his body but desperate questions and swishing curtains.

But I knew how to reach the inside of his room. Getting up on my tiptoes and peering into the window I could imagine myself invisible and slipping through the crack in the door's threshold. Once inside I put my face near his face and lifted his hand to touch the top of my head. With sheer force of will, I hovered over his bed so that what he saw was a vision of his own afterlife above him, some evocation reminding him to live, some reproach for him to look searchingly into the eyes of the spirit and become a man again in a way he hadn't been before.

Seated behind me that first night were some other people in the waiting room, but I don't remember their names or the reasons they were there, though I knew both at the time. One gentleman with a gray mustache held a briefcase over his lap but never opened it. He and my mother talked in low voices for a few minutes just before my brothers drove me back home late that night.

In his forties, my father was an athletic man with a handsome face like that of a navy lieutenant commander—which he was. A reservist, he would don his whites and report for duty down by the ship channel once a month on a Wednesday. His hair was dark with a sprinkle of gray, his small curls sheared close. His mouth was precise and gave the impression of always being about to smile. He was trim from running several miles a day and playing racquetball. It was his being struck in the head with the side of an opponent's racquet a few weeks earlier during a tournament at the downtown YMCA that likely triggered the aneurysm to burst.

It wasn't until three months later that my father was released from the hospital, and I listened to his muddled talk as if I were listening to a secret language for which there was only the code you created to break it. But it was still unbreakable. His voice was spooked, and the few words he could stutter and coax out of his mouth were spooked, too, and quickly evaporated or were thrashed in the air. It was now understood that I would do most of the talking when I was with him. Words would swoop from his brain to his mouth and then get trapped there. And then, the words would fall back, as through a trap door, into some unknown region of the brain. He confused my name with my brothers' names. But the names of objects, animals, plants, trees, streets, cities, people, even friends he'd known a lifetime over—these words eluded him like birds disappearing into the air. He was of course still an adult, a father, but he could hardly speak his own language and found the whole process of using his words a disturbing trial. There was a great labor in his effort to speak, and it came from a love of meaning so unlike what the poets talk about and so contrary to the arguments out there that language has no meaning. Once he wanted to talk to me about politics, which we enjoyed. He was trying to say something about the Soviet Union, and he just started calling the Soviet Union and anything having to do with what he perceived to be the communist menace "the red." I didn't get it at first, and then I did. Coming upon metonymy as his new way to talk, at least with those who were aware of this special shorthand—like "the red" for Soviet Russia—was like finding ways for language to pose for meaning rather than just be literally representative. The loss of language was irreversible. But metaphor, double-think, and the temptation to reanimate existence was not.

Just as Keats says that a "man is capable of being in uncertainties, Mysteries, doubts, without any irritable reaching after fact & reason," I was given an opportunity to learn that the unknowable must be comprehended every day. Even learning something new—or relearning something once known as my father was trying to do again with his use of speech—doesn't negate your sense of wonder. "The world is full of obvious things," Sherlock Holmes says in *The Hound of the Baskervilles*, which I was reading around the time my father got sick, "which nobody by any chance ever observes." This sense of being observant was the same with learning to listen and talk to my father. Before his illness there were words in the stream of his consciousness. He could see them in the currents of his mind as they polished themselves up into his mouth. The words were like maps of a life unfolded into being. Now the routes were more like labyrinths. He could neither retrieve the words nor put them back. All that floated there was the mystery. In the presence of all that, I discovered too that there are mysteries residing in the consciousness of my own mind that I don't want to get out of the way of. I was having a fresh understanding that pain and coming into consciousness are connected. As much as I might try to avoid the pain or face it, imagination alone would not bring—well, I didn't know what. Enlightenment? Maybe.

During this time in junior high school I had AV class

third period just before lunch. We were assigned to de-
liver film projectors and televisions and set them up for
the teachers. Once our assigned deliveries were accomplished—and before we had to retrieve the machines
again at the end of the period—there usually was time
in the AV room to listen to tapes or watch movies on our
own under the guise of making sure everything worked
okay. Whenever I could, I would plug in cassettes of fa-
mous speeches by John F. Kennedy, Robert F. Kennedy,
and Edward Kennedy, which I had taken to memorizing.
I knew all of JFK's 1961 inaugural by heart as well as some
lesser known speeches, like the one he gave in 1962 at Yale
University upon receiving an honorary degree that more
or less begins, "It might be said now that I have the best
of both worlds, a Harvard education and a Yale degree,"
and also his autumn 1960 acceptance speech to the New
York State Liberal Party. The highlight for me is his defi-
nition of liberalism:

> But if by a "Liberal" they mean someone who
> looks ahead and not behind, someone who wel-
> comes new ideas without rigid reactions, someone
> who cares about the welfare of the people—their
> health, their housing, their schools, their jobs,
> their civil rights, and their civil liberties—someone
> who believes we can break through the stalemate
> and suspicions that grip us in our policies abroad,

if that is what they mean by a "Liberal," then I'm proud to say I'm a "Liberal."

I memorized Bobby Kennedy's presidential announcement speech from the late winter of 1968: "I run to seek new policies—policies to end the bloodshed in Vietnam and in our cities, policies to close the gaps that now exist between black and white, between rich and poor, between young and old, in this country and around the rest of the world." And I memorized his speech from April 4, 1968, given extemporaneously in Indianapolis on the night Martin Luther King Jr. was assassinated, when Kennedy says:

For those of you who are black and are tempted to fill with—be filled with hatred and mistrust of the injustice of such an act, against all white people, I would only say that I can also feel in my own heart the same kind of feeling. I had a member of my family killed, but he was killed by a white man. But we have to make an effort in the United States. We have to make an effort to understand, to get beyond, or go beyond these rather difficult times. My favorite poem, my—my favorite poet was Aeschylus. And he once wrote:

*Even in our sleep, pain which cannot forget*
*falls drop by drop upon the heart,*

*until, in our own despair,*
*against our will,*
*comes wisdom*
*through the awful grace of God.*

What we need in the United States is not division; what we need in the United States is not hatred; what we need in the United States is not violence and lawlessness, but is love, and wisdom, and compassion toward one another, and a feeling of justice toward those who still suffer within our country, whether they be white or whether they be black.

And I knew by heart the conclusion of Ted Kennedy's eulogy for Robert given just a few months later at St. Patrick's Cathedral in New York City:

My brother need not be idealized, or enlarged in death beyond what he was in life; to be remembered simply as a good and decent man, who saw wrong and tried to right it, saw suffering and tried to heal it, saw war and tried to stop it. Those of us who loved him and who take him to his rest today, pray that what he was to us and what he wished for others will some day come to pass for all the world. As he said many times, in many parts of this nation, to those he touched and who sought to touch him: "Some men see things as they are and say why. / I dream things that never were and say why not."

I was inspired by the Kennedy legacy and that period of our nation's life as a time of great hope and achievement. I wasn't yet alive when John F. Kennedy was assassinated, and I was too young to remember Bobby Kennedy. But I think my own sense of what is possible in this country, part of the reason I became a writer, comes in part from memorizing those words and wishing to embody them in my own. But it was more than the political message I was responding to. The elegance of the Kennedy speeches must have allowed me to admire hope out of dark things, and to see that both hope and the dark things can be loved, even if, as Pablo Neruda says, they might be loved "in secret, between the shadow and the soul." From memorizing the Kennedy words and watching my father struggle to speak, I was learning that only if I were willing to risk everything could I find out how far I might go. I might only do that if I was willing to be vulnerable among the mysteries. There are mixed feelings in that assessment, but poetry would become a chance to find a clear expression for them.

# FROM THE EARTH
# TO THE STARS

I n August 1984 I finished last in the ten-meter platform at the United States Diving Championship in
Santa Clara, California. Greg Louganis, who'd won
two gold medals at the Olympics that summer, finished
first. Determined to return to nationals the following
year and—figuring I couldn't do worse—move up the
leader board, I went to Nashville for the summer of 1985
to train full-time.

It might have been my father who put the idea into
my head when I was seven years old—and he'd already
persuaded my older brothers, so I suppose I just wanted
to go with them—but for whatever reason I went to my
first diving practice in Houston at the community pool
near our house on Loch Lomond. The coach was Bill
O'Hearn, who was glad to have a little dweeb join his
summer team because in diving the earlier you start and
the longer you stick with it the better shot you have to
become competitive. In the fall we joined Nancy Duty's
competitive AAU team that trained at the pool at the old

Shamrock Hotel. Nancy was a South Texas girl from Brownsville. She had an angular face and a stocky, athletic body, and she dyed her hair a blood-orange red. In 1952 she missed qualifying for the Olympics by less than a point. The sting never healed. Nancy had trained at the Shamrock Hotel, too, and once she started coaching there she developed two Olympians and lots of national finalists. I would train with her until I left for college.

The grounds around the Shamrock's pool were lavishly landscaped, and one of the unique features of the ten-meter platform was its open spiral staircase. The pool was so big you could water-ski in it; at least that's what people said. Some time later Nancy took a job managing the pool at the Jewish Community Center, and most of her divers moved over there with her. It was a good move for me. The new outdoor pool was a short walk from my house along the banks of Brays Bayou. The JCC's outdoor pool was a Z-shaped deal with little shade, and the diving well comprised one of the doglegs. Most days during the school year I trained in the small indoor pool at the JCC in the afternoons, and then twice a day outdoors again in Houston's blistering summers. A typical week I might practice all totaled a thousand dives, even if in the competition I was training for I'd perform just eleven dives. That severe ratio between practice and performance—like drafts and publication—is weighted toward the former.

During the summers of my sophomore and junior

years in high school I went to Florida to train with Olympic coach Dick Kimball. Morning workouts with Kimball began at 7:00 a.m. and lasted until 11:00 a.m. We'd practice trampoline, jog three miles, do strength training and dry-board exercises, plus run through our elementary springboard dives and entries in the pool. This was followed by a two-hour afternoon workout of our difficult somersaulting and twisting dives, and for those of us who competed on the ten-meter platform, another workout in the evening three times a week. Saturday mornings we'd have an inter-squad meet. By the time I arrived at Boston University on a diving scholarship in the fall of 1982, I'd been diving on and off for eleven years in the blue days of summer and the dour, dull afternoons of winter too.

In Nashville I followed a similar routine as we had in Florida—morning practices, afternoon practices, platform in the evenings. My college coach, Jamie Greacen, had been an All-American diver at Harvard. From Connecticut and in his mid-twenties then, he looked a lot like the poet James Merrill—thin, tucked-in, ruddy, almost subdued. He was a geologist by training and was getting his masters in coastal erosion. His expression was reticent, and I suppose he was uncomfortable spending his initial years after graduating Harvard coaching college diving. Not that he appeared unhappy, but often I thought he believed he was confused by his own life and was just going along until he found more clarity.

As determined as I was to return to nationals, all that hot Tennessee summer I had a vague shadow inside me. I was aware of something resisting. Some of it was the intensity of training and the sense I might have reached a fatal plateau. But some of it was the long-distance relationship with Whitney back in Boston I was trying to keep up by writing letters every day. Writing letters like that involves unbelieving that physical proximity matters. At night after practice was over, I'd start a letter in the little room I'd rented. I'd write by hand with a soft blue pen and a legal pad of yellow paper. I'd seal the envelope and walk to the mailbox on the corner and return to the house. Sometimes all of that left me breathless and I'd have trouble talking even. None of my teammates or my coach knew for sure what was wrong with me, and after I denied my brooding meant anything, they simply stopped asking.

But I could feel something new and even natural happening as I wrote those letters and kept trying to make adjustments to feel that feeling again—the feeling of what, I wasn't sure. But I could feel my rib cage soften when I was writing and my heart would beat in a kind of rhythm. It was like something from Dvořák's "From the New World"—violins chopping and then the horns triumphantly on the march. Then the sensation would flag and my breaths would slow, and my body would take on a primitive fragility. It was like there was some breezy, folk, melodic rhythm inside me. Writing daily like that, feeling my ribs and heart, must have been a garish but tangible feeling of power. As if writing were a palpable weight.

Then I began to write the daily letters with more secrecy. They were too erotic to speak of, the physical act of the writing of them I mean. When I inserted myself into the process of writing it was like I was a cat crawling into the sentences and paragraphs. A similar sensation was happening to me when I was diving, too. When I'd be underwater after a dive, I could feel the air in my lungs build pressure, just as at night in my rented room I could feel the words in me build pressure. Kicking underneath the water in the deep end of the pool after a dive and before I'd swim back up to the surface, I felt as if I were haunting a maze of night and dreams. Underwater is as close as I've been to feeling what the unconscious might be like with its awful instinct and silence. Underwater you have no age. You feel—just thrown from the sky at least—weightless. It's like the thought, or the thought prior to, an utterance or an avowal, a surrender, and then deliverance.

In the air, too, diving is a sport of continual adjustments. You practice your moves and flips and twists, and you sharpen your kinetic prowess and your acrobatic finesse. And yet bouncing off the three-meter diving board or bounding from the ten-meter platform is like entering the foreign language of the air. You learn its accents, you figure out its currency, you develop the cadences of a native, but you are always a foreigner. Much as you develop routines and skills to master its idioms, you never succeed at feeling at home there, never feel like you do when you are standing back on the ground where you belong. When you're a diver, you're only a tourist of the air. Then, after you've plunged into the water and held your breath underneath the surface, you swim back up and quickly climb out of the water for the safety of the ground and the hot pool deck. It's an exotic joining of distances, like tracing a memory. Every dive I did, whether in practice or in competition, was a new beginning. Standing stoically on the diving board—before takeoff, arms dropped at my side, and reviewing the moves of the dive in my brain—it was as if I were simultaneously filled with the knowledge of everything I had learned in practice and also completely ignorant of what the future of the dive would actually bring.

Nothing so resembles the practice of adjustments, of risking and accepting failure, of pleading with yourself for redemption, like diving does as writing a poem. The one time I remember upsetting Jamie was during a dual meet one season in upstate New York against Syracuse. I was competing on the three-meter board. Right before one of my dives, as I had done before every dive of my life in every competition I'd been in, even in little inter-squad meets, I stopped next to my coach on the way to the diving board for some last-second guidance. Jamie must have sensed I wasn't listening as he gave me instructions about my head position or takeoff strategy or whatever it was. "Did you get that?" I hadn't and more or less said so when, while watching the previous diver set the board's fulcrum into place in the natatorium, I said, I'm just going to figure it out in the air. That was arrogant of me then. But the attitude of keeping some room in my imagination—in my heart, my mind—for the unimaginable would go a long way for me as a writer. I didn't know it at the time, but diving, and even the indeterminacy of the letter writing, was teaching me that every time I start a new poem, I'm having to learn to figure out how to write poetry all over again.

Things didn't turn out the way we had planned in Nashville. At the U.S. Diving Nationals qualifying meet, I missed the cut by a tenth of a point. Afterward I couldn't help but think of Nancy Duty and her lost Olympic dreams. Jamie and I—we'd planned to drive to St. Louis for the national championships—decided to skip Missouri altogether and drive cross-country to go backpacking along the Montana and Wyoming border near Beartooth Butte. Once on the road I couldn't keep up my letter-writing effort, and that all fell apart. I wouldn't see Whitney again until the Creeley reading at MIT.

I'd never known how much driving across America is like a beautiful dream. It's as if you're unconscious for four or five days as you surrender to the road, and you don't so much forget how to live as learn to live anew. Driving like that, crossing mile marker after mile marker under the long skies, is a kind of happiness, a prosperity of sheer energy. But I also didn't feel the happiness was mine. It was as if the happiness existed outside my body and I was stepping into it briefly and feeling some exalted transfiguration take place like a puzzle being decoded— much as it happens during writing. The road would hum beneath the little Volkswagen Scirocco we were in and break the spell, but I could still feel whirrs and whispers in my ears.

We let the miles take us in. They'd crinkle and re- lease. With the windows down, I'd lean against the doorframe and feel the rush of light. The sky above would become a dome of wind. At night we'd sleep in the open air of a state campground, and the stars would dot my brain. Jamie and I were in the process of evolving from coach-and-athlete to friends on that trip. Sitting side by side in the car we seldom looked at each other but, taking turns driving, we would watch the hours of horizon and the blurting landscapes as if following the sketches of a painting or the billows of the ocean. A lot of the time we listened to cassettes of the music Jamie had on hand—J. J. Cale and Little Feat, Johnny Cash and the Stanley Brothers, the Nitty Gritty Dirt Band. The music converted the trip into a light revision of daily life. We rehashed the failed competition over and over—you'd think if you get eights and nines on a front three-and-a-half, I kept saying, you're going to make the cut—until somewhere around Sioux Falls when we had nothing more to say about it. And that was that.

Once we got past the Badlands in South Dakota, we dipped up and down the interstate until finally arriving somewhere south of Red Lodge. The big sky of Montana wasn't so much full of promise as it was implicitly fleeting, and I understood the notion of fleetingness as much as I understood the meanings of those letters and the expression of a single dive that ends in the limits of light like the final note of a song or the farthest point you can see on a road. Looking into the sky from the car, it was as if my identity were being stripped away with the size of it all. In front of me was a new life.

We hiked two straight days into the Shoshone National Forest and made base camp near a narrow lake. One evening about dusk we were resting next to our small campfire. We were high above the backcountry and heard tromping on a hill up behind us. We scampered in that direction to take a look even though the sun was starting to set in long and coppery lingering layers and pink waves. Stars were already coming on directly above us too—"Non est ad astra mollis e terris via," I half-whispered a line from Seneca I'd memorized in high school Latin to Jamie, pointing his attention upward at the stars. "There is no easy way from the earth to the stars," I said. What we'd heard and found in a bright clearing was a herd of elk. We kept our distance.

Watching them we both felt a little exalted, perhaps blessed. Another dozen elk trotted through, followed by five or six more, then three more, then seven or eight. Elk after elk for twenty minutes continuously—and then I noticed the full moon now coming up big and fast in the east, just opposite where the light from the sunset was still waning in the west. The moonlight was casting a silver net over the narrow trees, forcing its way through the cracks between the branches.

We sat down on a boulder and looked at the unlikely moment beginning to overflow in front of us. The elk were moving through but not hurrying, just keeping pace, appearing before us and disappearing behind the trees again as if they were arriving and departing out of thin air, panting a little. The stars above us seemed tireless too, emerging like small bright heads of nails into the darkest part of the skies overhead. There were still glints of sunlight dappling the ground. I was feeling totally disarmed when suddenly I noticed in the far sky miles and miles to the north of us there was a lightning storm. The jags flashed and counter-flashed. It seemed as if the lightning was responding to the sun setting and the moonrise and the stars coming on and the elk in the clearing above the hill, and perhaps to Jamie and to me, too. If every shard of lightning roiling far off in the north sky was a reminder that I'd be separated from the earth one day, I doubt I thought it at the time. And yet I craved it and watched it all with great curiosity and wished I knew the words to describe what was happening. Or at least the questions to ask.

But even if I had known what questions to ask in that moment, there would be too many answers for me to comprehend. Some kind of truth was being offered, but it was an un-explorable truth, a mystery, like water, that no survey could completely map. None, but poetry, I started to think, years later, when I kept coming back to that experience scratching its claws in my mind. The elk had moved on, and the moon was higher, smaller, and the sunlight all but gone. But that moment in the Shoshones was an introduction to freedom and danger. Neither of us talked on the way back to camp under the darkness of the trees. What could I have been thinking, I wonder. That if there is something more to witness, I may never discover it? That confusion is also a small harbor from life or love? That failure is inevitable? That death might be disappointing?

Next morning we threw on some wood and re-started the campfire, lost in the transformation still of what had happened the night before. And lost in time, too, the way you lose track of time in the wilderness and where everything I understood previously about my life and the expressions I had to describe it seemed impossible to recover, and the absences impossible to fill, and I could feel all of the wilderness even inside my nose, and I could feel a knowledge come over me that I would always be able to breathe that wilderness even when

I was thousands of miles away, as if I were breathing hope and wetness and long weeds and dark branches. It was right about then, warming my hands by the fire, I suddenly realized my flight from Denver back to Houston was leaving in just two days. We packed up camp quickly and began to hike what we figured was a ten-hour downhill trek back to the trailhead where we'd left the car. If we were lucky, we could get to the car by nightfall and then drive all night down to Cheyenne, then south to Denver and make it to the gate with a few minutes to spare. All the day long we kept a fast pace, jogging when we came to the steeper downhill switchbacks.

Even if that was the whole story, and it's not, but even if it were, I would have taken so much from that experience on the mountain into my writing life, not least of which would be the idea that failure is not an unbearable shimmering and success is not an endless brightness. Our understandings of our experiences are sometimes shapeless. Like shadows, they move on. We might think we'd forgotten them entirely—and then we might, later in life, tread upon them again when a kind of uneven dust gets kicked up in our imaginations, dust fine as powder, but for a few hoof-prints still left behind like the spirit of a forgotten creature. This creature becomes a private archetype of forces we are unaware of. But they surround us always—even sitting in this room just now, writing this sentence, listening to the rattle of my pencil—just as they have with my forefathers so that we are always beset by temptation.

Meantime, hiking down to the trail, I noticed something worrisome in the offing. Behind us, to the north, in billowing layers in the skies, that thunderstorm from the night before was bearing down in our direction like a massive wave of disappointment. When we made it safely to the trailhead parking lot just as darkness was coming on, the rain fell finally down in a howling icy noise that seemed it might never come to an end. Because it was my flight to catch, I offered to drive all night in the blinding rain. About an hour in, as Jamie fell asleep, I caught up to a semi-truck rolling ahead of us. Like a guide through the labyrinth of the night of hard rain, that truck led me for six hours straight from midnight until dawn. Driving like that in tandem with the semi, wavering and withering together through the mountain passes, was a noble mystery of compatibility in silence and solitude. The slick highway and static vision from the rain became a new dream of peacefulness, a fragrant entrance into the mist of the soul, unlinked to all but the anonymous nomad cruising wearily in front of us mile after mile with unfolding compassion. It's the way with metaphor too, I would learn. It hides in random visible experiences like a dark suit pulled from the back of a closet found to still fit. I hid behind that trailer truck. Sometimes lost in myself during the few tenuous moments when the rain got so thick I couldn't find his taillights and had to switch in and out of the steep curves of the road alone, I became lost in a way that's like knowing the taste of life and all the while forgetting the absurd sensations and renunciations and grand banners where one weeps over nothing. In those moments I didn't even ask myself to exist but suffered joyfully in my newly created dream. When the truck ahead would slow around steep uphill curves of the highway to just ten miles per hour, so did I, keeping the little VW only a few feet off as the rain sloshed in the oars of the wipers. When the truck sped up to eighty-five miles per hour on the straightaways, I did too, punching it to keep his silent array at the edges of blurry vision. All night J. J. Cale was singing plaintive Oklahoma ballads inside the car—

> Jody May, she got a dollar
> Down the road you can hear her holler
> "Get up Clyde, we got something to do
> That old dog can sing the blues"
>
> He don't move, he don't flinch
> Clyde, he don't move an inch
> Just sit on the porch without no shoes
> Picking his bass and singing the blues

Near first light of morning, after the rain had finally eased and ceased, when the semi-truck turned toward

Cheyenne and the blue inner skies of my own mind returned, a strange serenity emerged that I could see and not see. It was like a vague feeling of dissatisfaction coming on. Just then my dear guide, my unknown Virgil of the all-night mountain roads, rolled down his window and raised his left arm high into the damp air to bid us farewell. He knew what I'd been up to all night for sure. Offering a long wave, he whomped his horn four times. I honked in reply, flashed the brights at him, and turned the little world of the Volkswagen in the other direction south toward Denver.

Back in Houston I made a visit to Nancy at the JCC's pool and told her I thought the following year would be my last as a diver. We were next to the gate that leads onto the pool deck, and I could see the opening to Brays Bayou in the thick August air. She was taking diet pills, she said, and talking up a new prospect that had joined her team the year before. Because she had to get to the deck to coach a workout, we had a short goodbye. The following spring at the NCCA Eastern Conference Championships at Harvard's Blodgett Pool back in Boston, I qualified for finals on three-meter, taking the last of eight spots. Finals consisted of three dives. Aware this would be my last competition, Jamie pulled me aside and said, dive for the elk. Climbing up the ladder to do my front three-and-a-half, I briefly thought of them emerging in waves on the hilltop as if out of a dream. And I thought of my months in Nashville too and my failure

at nationals the summer before. That failure was full
of arousal because I smoked that first dive for sevens.
Underwater, I felt transfigured, as if my body were one
submerged answer to the inconceivable wonder of living.
Then I did a reverse two-and-a-half also for sevens. And
finally for my reverse one-and-a-half somersaults with
two-and-a-half twists, my favorite dive and my most
difficult dive, I took off from the board and could sense
the blue water fall out beneath me and move far away
like a past life, giving me ample time to do the trick. I
could sense the crowd in the stands peeling away too in
a dry silence as my legs stretched out straight together
and pointed sharply down into my toes. I flipped and
twisted around once, twice, two and a half times, and—
says Larry Levis—it's "all or nothing in this life / . . .
Sweet nothing / Sweet, sweet nothing"—I squared it up
to where I could see the water coming fast and oriented
myself in the air like a compass needle. And then ripped
through the water without a splash. I stayed down underneath the water for as long as I could hold my breath
and felt the old life wash over me. I knew I nailed the dive
and didn't care about the scores. By the time I emerged
from underwater, the judges had tucked their scorecards
away.

Even then I knew writing was next. When that de-
cision to reorient my life came a few months later, I determined to use my years as a diver as a peculiar sort of
model for literary life—for training, for discipline, and

for patience. I'd been a competitive athlete on and off for fifteen years, and I knew it was time for me to retire. So I was determined to give myself fifteen years writing poems before I'd even begin to evaluate whether to keep going.

# NIGHTHAWKS

One night in Boston when the leaves had already gone red and yellow, bare and brown, one of the nighthawks screamed. The four of us—Giff, Nick, Paul, and I—had been living together for more than a year and were drinking beer on the hot roof above the apartment on Glenville Ave. We'd come up the fire escape at sunset—and from where we were on the rooftop, we could see a line of parked cars below snaking north against the curb—to watch the nighthawks loop overhead in squadrons of tapered gray slashes that delighted us.

But I'd never heard one scream before. At least it sounded like a scream, and I imagine now its mouth was open wide too. After it screamed it flew close to my face making the whizzing sound a truck makes when it roars by you on the road. The scream was not the usual, uncaged, harsh *peent*. Nighthawks we saw usually made alarming, nasal whistles. But this was a bright scream and then, just as suddenly, the nighthawk sizzled past us all again before taking a bat-like flip turn over to the trees in Ringer Park across Allston Street. Around that time I was reading a lot of Juan Ramón Jiménez and loved his poem "The Green Bird," that in the W. S. Merwin translation I had goes—

> *I have come.*
> *But I have left my lament*
> *at the edge of the sea*
> *weeping.*
>
> *I have come.*
> *But I will be of use to you in nothing*
> *Because it is my soul.*
>
> *I have come.*
> *But do not call me brother*
> *because my soul is there*
> *weeping.*

I told them all about the lines from Jiménez, and we talked about what we'd seen. Nick, who was dressed in khaki shorts, his straight hair covering his ears, said he could see its eyes looking at us and thought we must have done something wrong. But, I said, we'd never heard one scream before. A few nights earlier we'd counted thirty nighthawks overhead, the most we'd seen in one night. Paul offered the theory that our presence was hurting this one nighthawk. He expressed this with mock seriousness. And then he downed the rest of his beer. We're not doing anything special, Giff said, lying on his back with his legs crossed. He had a beer in one hand and a cigarette in the other. Giff was the birder among us.

We had moved to the edge of the deck now. The deck was made of wooden pallets, the kind you see in warehouses. We'd built the deck over a couple of days a few months earlier because the roof above 124 Glenville Ave.—flat with no railings—had a gray rubber surface that was, in the summers, too hot to stand on barefoot. More so we were concerned that some partygoer, drunk, high, or worse, would wander over to the edge of the roof and fall three stories to the pavement. We imagined the brutal headline: "Paralyzed Undergraduate" or "Coed Leaps to Death." One afternoon Giff and I asked the check-out guy at Brookline Liquor if we could have the wooden pallets piled out back next to the dumpster. You can't have them, he said as he rang up the beer. But if they go missing, I won't go asking about it, will I?

"Let's do some crime," one of the guys who lived above us said before he drove us over in his black Chevy van a few nights later after Brookline Liquor had closed up. We hauled some two dozen or more pallets up the stairs to the roof and then set about filling in the gaps with found pieces of board wood, battening them all together to make a platform deck about the size of a handball court. One evening with a dozen friends over and sitting on the deck, Jeff Smith brought his bicycle up to the rooftop and began making circles and figure eights. When he wouldn't get down, we ordered the entire party off the rooftop and left Jeff on his bike up there alone. I guess he stayed up on his bicycle alone for another few minutes and, he later told us, he only did that "until I felt sufficiently douchy enough to go downstairs."

The nighthawk was back now directly above our heads, and it screamed again. I was confused by the spectacle. It didn't seem to me the scream meant anything. But I took its call as a sign for something nonetheless, a thrilling, eccentric sort of sign. Maybe its meaning was erotic—I often had a predisposition to think mysterious things were erotic when I lived in Boston. Or, I thought, the scream just signaled the difference between shapes and words, like between the shape and meaning of *bird* and *bard*. The nighthawk kept rising and diving, a being within itself, like metaphor, that collapses or dies when you poke at it too much.

We knew enough not to be hypnotized by the nighthawk, but I couldn't help wanting to reflect about it. I so wanted to trust strange occurrences, like the screaming nighthawk, as more than what they were. I wanted to know for sure—though I never could know—that signs like this one kept our lives from being debased. The screaming nighthawk, I wanted to believe, could provide profound insights about aspects of human life. It just could. And the words I might come up with about the experience must have value too. And the meanings be-hind those words were something to pursue even if no words would come of it at all. The nighthawk could never be what I might think it stood for—whatever that was even, I hadn't a clue—I knew that. But I was still the beneficiary of it even if its meanings were in flux and the meanings were fleeting. I was in search of some substi-tute to stand in for the original experience, although I couldn't have described it like that that summer night on the rooftop above Glenville Ave. in Boston. We live in a moment, we have an experience, and we demand to understand what is happening. I believed that was true, just like a poem is the birth of something new, not an elegy of something dying, though it might include that. A poem is more than just its words just as the night-hawk screaming was more of—well, more of what I still wanted to know—than its voice. Again and again that night the nighthawk sizzled toward us in a white blaze of long wings. With the other guys I had sat down on the deck now, and then we were all lying on our backs. I be-lieve we were all watching the bird and the coming nights with a new obsessiveness.

# DRINK

For most of the people in Margaret Kennedy's
Latin classes at Bellaire High School in Houston,
language held the truth about existence—and existence, as they saw it, lacked meaning unless preserved
in history and literature. Language, ancient language,
was an opening to the mysteries and development of
thoughts, but at the same time a vague hindrance, depending on how you understood it. If learning to interpret the world could have a source tongue, we thought,
Latin was it. But Latin was difficult, hidden, and perplexing.

Mrs. Kennedy's classes were like being inside a Roman *scuola*. She considered the Pax Romana sacrosanct.
If she could have chosen a time to live in other than
the late 1970s in southwest Houston, she'd have chosen
something around the year 63 BC, when Cicero gave his
first oration against Catiline in the Roman Senate that
began with a series of blunt questions—

When, O Catiline, do you mean to cease abusing our patience? How long is that madness of yours still to mock us? When is there to be an end of that unbridled audacity of yours, swaggering about as it does now?

She didn't think of Latin as something fundamental, that's for sure. She was certainly not one of those brute classicists you imagine, slicing off your fingernails when you bungled a declension. It was more she treated ancient languages like fine bourbon. She made you want to come forward and drink. And I drank up Latin as Mrs. Kennedy offered it. At least I wanted to. I went to her classroom in the school's annex as if I were a pilgrim to Trastevere in Rome, as if given enough time I could navigate the seedy alleys of Venice blindfolded. I wanted to be immersed in the archeological dirt of my language, to become a member of a society of words. Even though I had been hearing and speaking Hebrew since I could talk, and as familiar a tongue as it was to me, I also never felt drawn to it. Where Latin seemed to exclude even those who studied it, I never felt shut out. There was a catch though, and one I had to hide from others. My circle of friends during high school saw the kids who took Latin as a little pretentious and believed that anyone who liked Latin (*loved it*, in my case) represented the epitome of smugness. I tried to wear my interest lightly as if to stride outside my own body, and would couch my attitude toward Latin as affection for Mrs. Kennedy and not wanting to let her down. Perhaps this doesn't really matter much now. But when you're trying to locate your imagination in a world in which your identity is supposed to be something else, every stake you spear into the ground does matter.

Besides, I was falling deeply in love with an ancient Roman poet's lover. I truly was. My sight-readings of Cicero's witticisms or my noodling around in Livy's elegies—or in Horace's longings for the simple peace of country life on his Sabine farm, or what Pliny thought of the races, or Virgil's pastorals—were of far less interest to me than the sweet, dirty poems of Gaius Valerius Catullus and the object of his (no, our) affection, Lesbia. More than any other poem of Catullus's in which he extols the carnality of the mind, I loved this one—

*Ode et am. Quare id faciam, fortasse requiris.*
*Nescio, sed fieri sentio et excrucior.*

*I hate and I love. Why do I feel this, you ask?*
*I don't know. But feel it and I am in torment.*

Without Catullus—and especially without Lesbia, paramour of paramours—Latin classes might have been just dull drills of conjugations, vocabulary quizzes, raunchy dramas about Roman emperors, and a series of iambic trimeters, Sapphic stanzas, and rhetorical textbook blobs for translation about what makes a good appetite or Cicero's anecdotes on Themistocles at the Battle of Salamis. It takes imagination to love the fact that Romans indicated future time in the first two conjugations by inserting a future-tense sign between the present stem and the personal endings, or that the present indicative and the future indicative of verbs of the third and the fourth conjugations, though not inherently difficult, could cause you as much trouble as any other thing in the paradigms of conjugation. These forms, Mrs. Kennedy reminded us from behind her slender wooden lectern at the head of the room, are among the most common, and a little extra effort invested in mastering these forms properly, she would say, will pay rich dividends. Then again, there was Lesbia.

There were all sorts of rumors about Mrs. Kennedy. We believed that when she traveled in Rome a few summers before she had sat all alone in some unknowable piazza just to enjoy shunning Italian men who'd pass by whistling at her. She would shun them, we believed, all the while declaiming Horace's "Carpe Diem." Maybe not. But she did tell the girls that when they travel to Rome not to wear a red dress in public, so there was that. Anyway the story fit her personality. In keeping the past alive, she exposed us to the present. With her disapproving eyes she could make you squirm, even if you felt certain your answers were correct. Latin had turned her into a glorified soul. She had martyred herself to roomfuls of

First Year stutterers. For others, like me, she was the incarnation of hope and offered us reasons to embrace the stories of life and their various meanings.

Mrs. Kennedy was in her late fifties, I'd guess, when I took all three years of her classes. Slight with low shoulders, slender, she had a look of practicality in her eyes. She liked to wear silk blouses, usually red or reddish, cut lower than the usual schoolmarm, and hooped earrings. When she spoke she seemed to chew her words into a whisper as if she were trying hard to hide some knowledge from us. If we kept listening, she would let us in. Some days she seemed not to be talking to us at all, but carrying on an ongoing conversation with Agrippa or Nero or Octavia. She exuded a skittering acquaintance with the occult. She could whistle about something scandalous in a text we couldn't quite translate. Dumb darlings, Mrs. Kennedy would say, and she would pout a little—her the sole, extravagant genius in the room, praising the genitive of the whole in a sentence, not just for being used after the neuter nominative and accusative of certain pronouns and adjectives, but as something that might heal wounds and bring balance between order and wildness. A vocabulary pairing like *patientia / patientiae* didn't mean endurance alone but represented a moment in our existence when something undiscovered could seize us, when something new has entered us and our feelings grow silent. She was a kind of remorseless insurgent on behalf of western civilization. I remember Mrs.

Kennedy telling us the vague details of Caligula's sexual exploits. And, too, she described, with great tenderness, how lonely Ovid was in his fatal exile in Tomis—"Sweet love of country held me"—and she seemed to walk back into these pictures of the past as a form of salvation. For her or for us, we couldn't be sure.

One afternoon during my senior year, I'd arrived in fifth period Latin with Jim Beam on my breath and tried to pass by Mrs. Kennedy's desk in the front of the room without her detecting it. I sensed she was onto me. It was spring semester, and all the windows were thrown open. Mrs. Kennedy was telling us that the Roman poets of the Augustan era must never be forgotten. Horace, Catullus, Virgil, Propertius were revolutionaries. I remember she told us that their poems would always be with us, that we could always enter them as if entering a dangerous life. When she said *dangerous*, she appeared to look at me. But she said the poems were not like life. You had to go to them, into them, to catapult yourself into their continuums. She quieted the room when she got philosophical like this, and at about that moment I could feel the tingle of bourbon right up into my teeth and gums. Language prays, she suddenly blurted. It prays! And do you know what it prays in? She again looked in my direction. I was just tipsy enough to know what she was getting at. In poetry, I wanted to say but didn't. She looked at me with a kind of slap of the eyes. It's salvation, she said. For a moment I felt that Mrs. Kennedy had explained life to me. Be it Latin or poetry, or whatever it was—I was feeling woozy by then. If I couldn't love what I was reading, I took it, it was better to have never read at all. But that couldn't be it.

She had moved away from the front of the room after telling us we could have the rest of the period to work on our homework. Students appeared to me to be wavering left to right in their seats now, and when Mrs. Kennedy walked across the room back to her desk, I thought I could hear the floors cracking. The whole business of poetry and life felt suspended suddenly as if Mrs. Kennedy were manipulating the topographies of the future. I was relieved the windows were open. Outside the air smelled of dirt and you could already sense the failures of springtime. It was nearly ninety degrees out there. That was the best Houston had to offer in May, a kind of painful joy of hot air. I could hear a few students in the open corridor talking, and beyond them a Trans Am with its windows down and the radio turned up. It was something country western but of the countrypolitan variety—tambourine with a brute backbeat. It was the kind of music that made you want to forget everything, as if you could exist beyond the body. I looked back down at my Latin papers. Whatever it was, the mysterious words were beautiful in a wholly different way. They emitted the rhythms of my life, and like the rhythms of life you might not always remember them, but you never forget them either.

# TEXAS ROSES

When my family moved from Tulsa to Houston in 1968, we lived for a short period on Lymbar Drive in the southwest corner of the city across the Chimney Rock ditch from Johnston Junior High. Shortly after, we moved north to Loch Lomond on the other side of Braeswood Boulevard, where I was given a room in the corner of the house that overlooked rose bushes my mother planted. They were generally tidy roses, sometimes raucous, and often there'd be petals scattered on the square brick patio. They had a kind of capricious beauty. When the porch light was left on overnight outside my window, I would look at them in the glare to help me fall to sleep.

William Faulkner writes that beauty "means the scent of roses and then the death of roses." My experience was more limited, but I liked to stare at those roses all the same. There might be something to them having an elegiac consciousness because I began having a recurring dream about that time, too. This would have been when I was in elementary school. I'd dream of plunging into seawater and then, alternately, chased on land around a dense, circular garden by something unknown. Sometimes the dream felt like an experience, and other times it was limited to scenes or brief acts. The dream felt like I was always leaving home and unable to return. Or always returning and unable to arrive. I'd come to a point where I couldn't go any farther and could barely lift my arms they'd feel so weighted down. My legs felt like they were sunk into sand, and no matter which direction I'd run I'd be returned again to the start.

The dream sometimes began with joy and then would turn to expectation and illusion. There'd often be a point when I'd be sure I'm about to drown in the sea—and then the running me, the one who is being chased, emerges out of the water. Or the running me who is about to be caught by the pursuer dives into the sea and begins to swim. It's as if I'm regressing into my animal instinct, into a pre-human madness. The dream could even feel a little funny, like imagining eating raw meat with a fork. And there'd be grunting while I was running or swimming. The grunting would go on as I felt myself kicking against the water or running on the gravel, and then a swilling growl would come upon me, and then snatching at comings and goings, swimming toward or away from whatever was approaching, running toward or away from something falling just out of reach. Now I can see I was simply existing in that recurring dream somewhere between being and unbeing, when everything that is radiant becomes all that you are able to praise. There was that, but I also feel the dream was a yearning for solitariness. It became, when I thought about it, an investigation of myself, what I might now think of as an exploration of identity, a kind of haunting of an ill-defined destiny. Or maybe just an old-fashioned interest in loneliness. It all happened in just the way obsessions obsesses us. Sometimes in the dream I would try to keep the vision going and not wake up, even though I'd be frightened and tired as I was chased around the garden, out of breath, running hard from the pursuer. And even though I'd want to awake—I could tell the difference, I knew I was dreaming—even in the last stages of the dream I'd try not to awake or to escape, but to return back into the dream.

When finally I awoke, I'd be just fine in my bed in the corner of the house with the pleasant rose bushes outside the window. Rattled, like a pinball, mildly out of breath but just mildly, and feeling a little wrecked, I'd pull up the sheets and blanket to my chin. When later I started to write my first poems I would think of the dream as an emotional prompt. I would get myself into that demolished place in my psyche with all that water splashing around and the footsteps of the pursuit just outside my hearing range, and I'd get at the feeling that my imagination was a kind of enemy, a pursuer, something to be feared, even hated. It was all so ordinary, that feeling, if strange too. I'd try to recreate the dream in my mind, even risk being destroyed by it. But I could never get the details to line up right.

A writer is often trying to answer a dream like that, answer imagination, and to understand one's self. But the images show you just enough of themselves to be close to you. And yet, they are not reachable. They show you just enough not to drown in them or be chased down. My first attempts to write when I was living in tiny Brownsville, Vermont, in the late 1980s had only a slight physical connection to the recurring dream I'd had back in Texas in the 1970s. But the recurring dream was still visible to me, and I could sense that it used to exist. It was like the memory of a touch on the arm from someone you wanted to be touched by. But all the desire for that touch happened so long ago that it seems to you an impossible fact of your own existence. And so when I first began to write I tried to chase that dream on the page as if I were chasing a piece of paper blowing down a staircase. It was like a blurry forgetting of all the elements. Like an ache you know is going to return. What was left was just the race toward the whatever it was as it was bouncing away—like chasing a balloon caught in the wind and the string with a ribbon attached to the balloon was just out of reach—and sometimes it felt as if I were gaining, and other times falling back. It would all go back and forth like that, and all I could gather was the littlest thing about the experience.

On rare occasion when I was older I had the dream again—every few years or so. I'd find myself back underneath the water, the waves sometimes strong, other times not, and I'd be swimming in a hurry. The undertow would be holding me down. And then I'd be floating to the calm surface. And then suddenly I'd be trying to abandon the garden again, running—almost in place with my heavy legs stuck in sand—from whatever anonymity was chasing me. All the while I'd be chased around in slow circles on the gravel path. However now when I awoke I'd feel some of the terror sticking around in my conscious life. The air would feel unpleasant. Other times I could still actively keep the dream going even throughout the daytime, as if the soul of the dream could exist outside the body and swayed in the offing. Writing would come to have that kind of fascination. I'd linger over the page rolled tightly into the typewriter just to see what must be put there. I'd find the salty taste of the watery place again on that page, and the dense garden, too. I'd lift my shoulders and chest—just as in swimming—as I'd lean into the typewriter keys. Words would open to me. I could hear the phrases and passages come clacking out of the typewriter just as I heard the pursuer. Not heavy footsteps but a fleet pursuit and a palpable panting. I might at first hesitate to try to see what I am writing, but then I'd worry I'll miss the point—just as in the dream I feared I'd get chased down and caught. So I'd get back to hammering away on the typewriter's stiff keys and keep up the inky throbbing.

What is to be said, I wonder now, about writing's capacity to prevent you the chance to check on your own whereabouts? When it's going well you don't worry if you're okay or if you're breathing. You simply keep your eyes open and cast downward. Danger doesn't occur to you. You believe you can breathe underwater. You believe you can outrun a strong wind or whatever it is behind you gaining speed. All along you're not even trying to get the point of what it is you're doing. And as you write, as in a dream, you can see your own body. You can speak in a clear voice. You can tread water or rest atop a brick wall as if leaning against loneliness, and you can catch your own eye looking at yourself there—even if there's nothing tender or maudlin or visionary about it. It's a matter of self-composition: Keep concentrating—then take a breath and hold it—and do it again. Your chest lifts, your nostrils inhale, your eyes narrow toward a threshold up ahead as you keep up your typing. You can feel the nakedness of your body in moments like that. There's a thrumming around you and behind you. Something unknowable, like the smell of love and death, and plain as the petal of a flower.

# DEFEAT

For a short time the summer before my senior year in college, I had nowhere to go but Houston. So I moved back in with my mother. The last place I wanted to be was in my old neighborhood of Meyerland, even for a few weeks. I had been living in Boston, and I was different now. To return home seemed like a defeat.

I had always seen Meyerland as an idyllic area of southwest Houston with its cozy, mid-century Tudor and colonial ranch houses. In August the wide roads and trim lawns had settled low against a tall sky. Now, after living in Boston, I couldn't see it at all anymore. Driving down Chimney Rock Road with the bulbous trees heavy under the long, humid skies was like a familiar dream. I did it without looking, without interest. I could only remember my childhood there but could not see who I was, even in so familiar a place.

I stayed alone most days in the air-conditioned house and buried my head in books. One was John Steinbeck's

*Travels with Charley*. His descriptions of Texas seemed right to me:

> I have said that Texas is a state of mind, but I think it is more than that. It is a mystique closely approximating a religion. And this is true to the extent that people either passionately love Texas or passionately hate it and, as in other religions, few people dare to inspect it for fear of losing their bearings in mystery or paradox. But I think there will be little quarrel with my feeling that Texas is one thing. For all its enormous range of space, climate, and physical appearance, and for all the internal squabbles, contentions, and strivings, Texas has a tight cohesiveness perhaps stronger than any other section of America. Rich, poor, Panhandle, Gulf, city, country, Texas is the obsession, the proper study, and the passionate possession of all Texans.

Houston was a segregated city, like most of Texas as a whole. Some of it by law, but most by tradition or fear. A lot of that was concealed from me as a child, but it wasn't like I didn't notice. For sure I was deeply in love with the city's eccentricities: oversized Lone Star flags that flew above gas stations and car dealerships, spaghetti-bowl freeways and pickup trucks, horizontal skyscapes, bulbous clouds, and fat belt buckles. The all y'all's, the honeys, and sweetie pies—I adored, took to heart. And the very best were the beautiful cowboy boots, central to a Texan identity. And everyone talking like they were just seconds away from doing a little cattle roping, even if most of the friends I knew from the Jewish Quarter of the city would go on to become ear, nose, and throat doctors, CPAs, money managers, insurance executives, lawyers.

I'd wanted to take my first poetry workshop my senior year of college but hesitated when I found out I would need to submit poems to get in. Problem was, I hadn't written any. I was only at that time still just imagining writing poems. Poking around my bedroom, I found a couple of high school literature textbooks I hadn't returned. Included there were Top of the Pops poems in English from across the centuries. There were Scottish ballads like "Sir Patrick Spens" and "Edward, Edward," John Donne's "Batter My Heart, Three-Personed God," Robert Herrick's "Delight in Disorder," John Milton's "Lycidas." I loved all these poems. Plus ones by Andrew Marvell, Henry Vaughan, Blake, Wordsworth, Shelley, and Keats. There was Whitman and Dickinson and Frost and Stevens and Dr. Williams. There was Hardy's "My Darkling Thrush" and W. B. Yeats's "Sailing to Byzantium." Plus: Walter de la Mare's "The Listeners," T. S. Eliot's "The Love Song of J. Alfred Prufrock," W. H. Auden's "Musée des Beaux Arts," Theodore Roethke's "My Papa's Waltz," Dylan Thomas's "Fern Hill."

It never occurred to me to try to write poems without the guidance of earlier poets and poems. Until that time I had only jotted down words and odd phrases, bits and pieces of overheard language, in a small notebook. I'd kept a journal of some kind, on and off, since I was in elementary school, beginning when I'd started a little newspaper in third grade called *The Spieler*. I published three issues of *The Spieler*—and wrote most of the articles myself. There was reporting on what happened in dodge ball at recess and after-school sports, plus interviews with my friends about their favorite super heroes. There were reviews of new movies and opinion pieces about the city's sports teams. There were limericks and short stories. You could say my mother was the *The Spieler*'s managing editor. The two of us would sit in the kitchen together in the evening after the dishes were put away, and she would read my hand-written articles and type them up on thin, inky duplicate paper. Mother took to the task somewhat reluctantly. It seems to me it took a lot courage for her to raise sons. I could feel, sitting next to her in the kitchen, that it made her unhappy that I was a separate being, apt to get myself into dangers, apt to disappear. And so she created a heavy circle between us, inside which there was often some shrapnel of suspicion. She had gathered her past into a kind of spirit pain, and even though she mothered with all her body and heart, she did so in a way that prevented you from wondering about her own dreams.

In the kitchen, though, it was clear it made her happy for a few hours that we were focused on this one thing together. She typed up my newspaper articles on her Selectric, and all through the house you could hear the speedy clack of the typewriter's keys and the motor's hum. You could hear the exasperation in her voice, too, insisting that I edit every page by hand in pencil and correct the misspelled words, which I did by looking them up in the blue Webster's dictionary she'd received as a high school graduation present. Her voice was a prod to move, but I understood that its intent was to instruct. To be correct was true to her journey. It's where she made her stand. As the two of us worked over *The Spieler* word by word, I must have taken it that a writer's job is not complete without attention to precision. In her mind, I suspect, she hoped the effort would lead to a worthwhile profession.

That's all the writing I did other than letters, which I loved composing and sending to friends. Throughout high school and into college my little notebooks, kept in a knapsack, had scribblings of ideas I never returned to. Things like—

*Write about watching Orion.*
*Write about driving on Galveston Beach at night*
*with one arm out the window.*
*Write about the genius of Dave Brubeck . . . of*
*strike 'em out, throw 'em out double-plays.*

*Write about cafés late at night and bars before*
  *noon.*
*Write about the color of wind.*

I can see now that these notes were the implicit beginnings of training myself to observe the world directly and the times I was passing through. Meantime the requirement to submit a poetry sample to get into that college workshop I took seriously. I would stow away in my bedroom and read samples of poems from the textbooks over and over. Then I'd try to imitate them. I loved Walt Whitman's elegy to Lincoln, "When Lilacs Last in the Dooryard Bloom'd," for the way it made me want to write about the Kennedy assassinations. I copied by hand poems by Dickinson and Keats and Hardy. I committed to memory five or six poems in those few weeks, including sections of the long lilac elegy by Whitman that begins—

*When lilacs last in the dooryard bloom'd,*
*And the great star early droop'd in the western sky*
  *in the night,*
*I mourn'd, and yet shall mourn with ever-returning*
  *spring.*

*Ever-returning spring, trinity sure to me you bring,*
*Lilac blooming perennial and drooping star in the west,*
*And thought of him I love.*

It seemed to me these poets had over-inflected their faith in sentimentality. They could be brilliant, they could be spurred on by the magic of the imagination, but their wisdom was questionable. And yet I understood and took close into my heart also what Walt Whitman says about grief, that it is the starting point of understanding our existence. I wondered what Mrs. Kennedy might say about contemporary poetry—well, what I took to be contemporary. I pulled out my Latin translations and began to reacquaint myself with Catullus and Virgil and Horace. Reading back and forth between the Augustan poets of Rome and the romantic and modernist poets of England and America, I suddenly began to lose sight of the connection among them all. There was a fracturing, and I felt forced to choose between what I knew and what I dreamed about.

Most nights during that summer's visit home I would drive across town to Mark Solis's house. He lived with his mother south of the Third Ward near MacGregor Park about half an hour east from Meyerland, in what was then predominantly the Hispanic Quarter. We were friends in high school, and had stayed in touch through correspondence. Mark was a fire hydrant of ideas about art and literature. When he spoke about his latest pleasures and opinions on music and literature and the movies, he shifted between a high squeal and a whisper. One night we were sitting in his living room where the little air-conditioner in the window sputtered while his mother messed around in the kitchen. Because she called him *Mijo*, I'd always called him that too. Mark wanted to be a novelist and had determined that summer to read fiction and poetry only in Spanish. I remember one night he was proclaiming his love for Lorca and García Márquez. I hadn't read them yet. Another night it was Neruda and Borges. He was telling me how these guys could see the crooked, warped indentations of the earth. García Márquez, he was saying, can make water dissolve with his writing. He moves beyond intention, Mark was saying, and he shapes out of thin air what had once been lost. And Borges, he goes—lighting a cigarette now and stretching his legs out across the long vinyl couch, and with his other hand smoothing over his thin brown mustache—Borges never hurries. His writing is tireless, but he's always panting. His stories emerge—Mark was saying, and now leaning closer to me so he could whisper—from the wilderness. Borges's words—Mark was wrapping up now, he was leaning his head back against the wall—are like dapples of obscurity.

Slow down, Mijo, I said—dapples of obscurity? He sat up again and squealed with a kind of rapture: Dapples, man. Blotches. Speckles. I said, I'll show you dapples. Have a listen to this Whitman, I said. I stood up and began reading all of part two of "Song of Myself." I was pacing around the living room now; then I moved into the kitchen before heading out the sliding glass door that looks onto the porch in the backyard. With Mark following me into the hot night air, I went on, gesturing and reading—

*Houses and rooms are full of perfumes, the shelves*
      *are crowded with perfumes,*
*I breathe the fragrance myself and know it and like*
      *it,*
*The distillation would intoxicate me also, but I shall*
      *not let it.*

*The atmosphere is not a perfume, it has no taste of*
      *the distillation, it is odorless,*
*It is for my mouth forever, I am in love with it,*
*I will go to the bank by the wood and become*
      *undisguised and naked,*
*I am mad for it to be in contact with me.*

*The smoke of my own breath,*
*Echoes, ripples, buzz'd whispers, love-root, silk-*
      *thread, crotch and vine,*
*My respiration and inspiration, the beating of my*
      *heart, the passing of blood and air through my*
      *lungs,*
*The sniff of green leaves and dry leaves, and of the*
      *shore and dark-color'd sea-rocks, and of hay in*
      *the barn,*

The sound of the belch'd words of my voice loos'd to
    the eddies of the wind,
A few light kisses, a few embraces, a reaching
    around of arms,
The play of shine and shade on the trees as the
    supple boughs wag,
The delight alone or in the rush of the streets, or
    along the fields and hill-sides,
The feeling of health, the full-noon trill, the song of
    me rising from bed and meeting the sun.

Have you reckon'd a thousand acres much? have
    you reckon'd the earth much?
Have you practis'd so long to learn to read?
Have you felt so proud to get at the meaning of
    poems?

Stop this day and night with me and you shall
    possess the origin of all poems,
You shall possess the good of the earth and sun,
    (there are millions of suns left,)
You shall no longer take things at second or third
    hand, nor look through the eyes of the dead, nor
    feed on the spectres in books,
You shall not look through my eyes either, nor take
    things from me,
You shall listen to all sides and filter them from your
    self.

That's dapples of "scurity," Mark says. Scurity? What the hell is "scurity"? We were both outside now, sitting in lawn chairs. We could hear the freeway traffic, late birds, crickets. The air had cooled into the eighties. Mark was fingering a joint and then passed it over. Yeah, *obscurity* you can't find, but "scurity" you can because it overflows. You shall listen to all sides, man, he was repeating one of the lines he liked. He says, those aren't obscure sides, are they? He was leaning close and whispering again. Our legs were practically touching. So what are they? Now we were practically touching our foreheads together, and I said, those are 'scure sides, Mijo. He really made no sense, but it was perfectly clear too. He leaned back into the lawn chair and chuckled, fished in his pocket for another cigarette. It was so fun to talk about writing this way. Mark took the Whitman from me and sight-translated part three into Spanish. We went on like that until the late passages of the poem, English and then Spanish, for over an hour, with all the dapples of Walt Whitman.

One afternoon late in August, just before I returned to Boston, the movie *Conrack* came on Channel 39. Set in 1969 and based on Pat Conroy's memoir *The Water Is Wide*, the movie details the experiences of a young teacher, played by Jon Voight, who takes on the fifth through eighth grades in a black school on an island off the coast of South Carolina. Conrack—the name his students give him because they can't pronounce Conroy—is shocked by his students' ignorance. None can add two plus two or count to six. None knows the name of the country they live in or the state. He's put off by the tough black woman principal, Mrs. Scott, played by Madge Sinclair, who tells him, "Treat your babies stern, treat 'em tough. Put your foot on 'em and keep it there."

In time Conroy has the students learning about Beethoven and the pyramids, human anatomy, Willie Mays. He teaches them to swim and takes them on their first Halloween across the river through the white neighborhoods of Beaufort. The movie's theme of accepting the burden of a white southerner in a rapidly changing world resonated with me easily back home in East Texas. The film opens with a montage of Conroy waking to classical music in his tidy Beaufort apartment contrasted with one of his future students, a black girl of thirteen years named Mary, played by Tina Andrews, waking up over on the segregated island in a wooden shack that's about the size of a large outhouse and built over a marsh. What inspired me was Conroy's intention to seize each new day as a journey into the mysteries of human experience. "Gather your rosebuds while ye may," he declaims to his students, and I realized that was what I needed to do, too. Gather your rosebuds while ye may. When late in the film Mary tells Conrack that a man on the island has asked to marry her, he dismisses the whole idea of that future life for her. Surprised and hurt, she retorts, "Why you always picking on me?" Because, says Conrack—

The gospel of according to Conrack is "I will. Higher. Stronger. Faster. Better. Not a floor-scrubber but Wanda Landowska. Not a diaper-changer but Marion Anderson. Not a pig-slopper but Mary McLeod Bethune. Not a fry-cook but Eleanor Roosevelt. *"Aut Caesar, aut nullus"*—that's Latin—"Either a Caesar or nobody."

When Conroy gets fired by the school district for his supposed radicalism, he drives his green van through the streets of segregated Beaufort and, speaking through a bullhorn, declares his limitations:

Ladies and gentlemen, I don't mean to take you away from your daily routine. I know you've got stores to open, clothes to wash, marketing to do, and other chores. But I just lost my job and I want to talk. My name is Pat Conroy. I was paid $510 a month to teach a bunch of kids on a little island off this coast how to read and write. I also tried to teach them to embrace life openly, to reflect upon its mysteries, and to reject its cruelties. The school board of this fair city thinks that if they root out troublemakers like me, the system will hold up and perpetuate itself. They think as long as blacks and whites are kept apart, where the whites get scholarships and the blacks get jobs picking cotton and tomatoes, with the whites going to college and

---

blacks eating moon pies and drinking Coca-Cola, that they can weather any storm and survive any threat. Well, they're wrong. Their day is ending. They're the captains of a doomed army, retreating in the snow. They're old men. And they cannot accept a new sun rising out of strange waters. Ladies and gentlemen, the world is very different now. It's true this town still has its die-hards and nigger-haters. But they grow older and crankier with each passing day. When Beaufort digs another four hundred holes in her plentiful graveyards and deposits there the rouged and elderly corpses and covers them with the sandy low-country soil, the Old South will be silenced and not heard from again. As for my kids, I don't think I changed the quality of their lives significantly or altered the fact that they have no share in the country that claims them, the country that's failed them. All I know is I found much beauty in my time with them.

Later that night in Mark Solis's backyard—crickets, cars burning rubber outside the Third Ward, squeals of horns, growl of pickup trucks, the low-nineties weather hard against the skin, aroma of cayenne and cumin, smoked beef, and red rice from the kitchen where Mark's mother was cooking again—I repeated the last sentence of Conroy's oration to Mark: "All I know is I found much beauty in my time with them," I said.

After a silence I added, I want that. I told him I was sure that's where my life was headed. I realized too that I would have to leave Texas and wished I could have managed my life differently and stayed there. That's a whole other story, but there was no doubt in my mind that I wanted to go.

Mark went to his room and brought back a copy of something by Pablo Neruda and then read some lines to me in Spanish:

> Adelante, salgamos
> del río sofocante
> en que con otros peces navegamos
> desde el alba a la noche migratoria
> y ahora en este espacio descubierto
> volemos a la pura soledad.

What's that in English, I asked, taking the book from him and thumbing for the page. He knew the lines by heart—

> Go ahead, get out
> Of the suffocating river
> with the other fish swimming
> from dawn through the journey of night
> and in this discovered space
> fly to a pure solitude.

# NOT THAT TOWN

From the time he arrived in America at the age of thirteen, my grandfather Joe Borg had wanted to start to live. So far his life had been a series of endings, and he hoped—he kept telling me, at least, for there can be no memory without one's own presence— that this time he could have a new quiet and new beginning all to himself and then make some money. He says this to me in 1927 about the time he leaves northern Iowa by train to live in Brooklyn near his father's sister, our Aunt Esther, for a few months when he was, in my memory, around the age of twenty. A young man now he was built like a fire hydrant, low to the ground—I know that much. I can see us heading out into Williamsburg together to find an apartment. We were taking a look at this tenement or that one, each of them narrow and shabby, and the rooms about the size of postage stamps. When we found one not far from Aunt Esther's apartment it was a fifth-floor walk-up, but we didn't care. We didn't intend to turn it into a home. After handing over the first month's payment to the landlord and putting a few towels on the floor for bedding, we moved in.

Joe believed he was too restless and ambitious for bucolic Elma, Iowa, anyway. The dark intervals of silence of Elma's days and nights had taken their toll. New York City was to be his rebirth. But after a few days in his fifth-floor walk-up, he felt lonely. And just as his own father had done when he first lived alone in America in Elma back in 1910—for ten years alone while his wife and sons were back in Ukraine—Joe began to talk to himself for company. He talked to himself about how this loneliness was something to overcome. His voice at first had come forward softly, as if the sounds were afraid to be touched by light. Then his words would find some Yiddish-built guttural wind in his voice. The words would break apart like ice on a river in springtime, shifting from destitution to sweetness. He would speak of the shadows and windows and stairwells. His voice would bounce off the walls of the small flat not in images but in spirits of the past. It was like his voice was drawing the paintings of Chagall into the room's air. He would speak to avoid his own confusion. The words of his sentences would cover the floor, not with Elma but Cherniostrov. He would talk of wheat fields on a summer afternoon, autumn in a village with a big sun above a house, a bridge, a butcher, a cemetery gate where those who had once lived together would finally flee together. Like Adam and Eve, he'd say, they'd departed the garden.

He would stop talking sometimes, suddenly, as if he heard footsteps approaching the door. Quietly he would whisper about the moon through the curtains. And then go on with his talking—he would tell stories about clowns at night and a fisherman's family. He would hum a song about fruits and flowers and King David with a smile spreading across his face. Often he would talk of peasant life. He would make portraits of his father and brother and young sister, born an American a few years earlier in Iowa, of his mother whose realness could not be shattered. Late at night, before drifting to sleep on the floor, while he could still hear the family below moving about in their late-evening business, he would speak of a single blue face he'd seen once in hedgerow on Broadway on his way home returning from work. It was evening, and the sun was beginning to set. A voice spoke to him from the hedgerow—a woman's voice, he said, that sounded like wind through the small leaves of bushes. He had noticed that the woman with the blue face's eyes were closed. The woman spoke of willow trees and abandoned towns. She described a hobo who called her *Mother*. Joe smiled. *Mudder*, he'd say, in his Yiddish accent, imitating the hobo. He spoke of the hobo return-ing to his tent on the edge of town. Joe's voice would play with things like that. And then he'd return home inside his head, and he'd drift to sleep.

After all his trials and travels, he'd say, after slipping across the Ukrainian border by boxcar with his mother and younger brother, after arriving in America without a lick of English and meeting his father and starting school in Elma in the first grade at the age of thirteen, and while holding down small jobs in town—lighting the fire in the school's furnace before hours, sweeping the floor at the grocer's at night, peddling rags and mismatched suits and trousers, collared shirts and vests, and pieces of scrap iron on the narrow bumpy Iowa blacktops—he now would have to confront his loneliness. Life, he'd say, was a series of broken rhythms, and all you could do was try to put the rhythms back together again. No matter what had shattered before you, he'd say to me in the little room, all you can do is overcome it. What other choice do you have? He had a writer's sense of persistence.

He was on the outs with his father about that time, too. It wasn't over one thing. But, Joe wondered, with all the trouble he'd given his father in Iowa—he'd lived with him for less than half his life, that's right, Joe would say, stabbing the air—perhaps even that was better than feeling lonely. But Elma was lonely too, he said out loud. Then stopped as if he could hear footsteps again at the door.

That loneliness was different, I said to him. It was a spring night, and we were walking up Union Avenue in a pleasant breeze as the Brooklyn houses and streets exhaled down to the river. Back there in Elma, I said, the world was so small. I had to fill it, he says. No distractions there, I said. But, he says, it just tempted you to disobey. We would bicker like that. He didn't give you any quarter. I suggested we paint the walls of the apartment green, like the color of new cornstalks. He gave me a look. Blue, he says, a dark blue like the color of the tallis bag where he kept his prayer shawl and *t'fillin*. With a couple of white stripes, he says. I wasn't having any of it. That would have been a disappointment to me, I said, as if the Old World could never be escaped from. This is America, I said, you could paint it pink and gray and yellow and black and brown. Blue, he says. We will paint it blue.

But we didn't paint the room, and the loneliness remained white as a sheet of paper until it became more of a celebration of solitude. The difference between solitude and loneliness matters for a writer, and learning to determine and manage the difference began for me in that little walkup during the 1920s. When I began to write, I was able to sense which was which, and I could go back to his fifth-floor flat anytime and not be shocked. That room without pretense or a bed was a place for me to think. No matter how far ago now in time it was that we lived there, I can always stand in front of the kitchen sink and can hear Joe as if he might be coming up the stairs from a day working at the warehouse or coming in from the gym where he'd been in the boxing ring. The dishes would be in the sink, but there was no food in the cupboards. Even now I can see our blankets sunk in the corner of the room, the corners of the unfolded towels askew, a small indentation sculptured into the pillow. Years can go by when I've forgotten that room. The dream of that time won't open up, and I assume the dream is broken. Then I reach up to the memory's handle and pull at it. Just like that, I pull on it, and it comes out like a Murphy bed easily enough. And I can write again.

Joe disliked that kind of musing, and he'd say so. He'd say, Bub, why are you making the present and the past so intermingled? I came to America with my mudder and brother Irving, I met my father, I worked as a rag peddler. Now I'm in New York. Next I'll leave New York, I'll meet your grandmother, I'll sell some hides, grease, a little scrap, and that'll be that. Life wasn't some kind of art form for him. It was a truth he'd already caught. He felt looking back at it wasn't going to change anything except make you feel tired. Even in his loneliness he didn't dwell on the past.

But his disinterest fueled my own, and it became like a secret hiding place where all the voices, like a dog barking in the night, come back or like an old man saying, Look, I've been where you are going. Thinking of his past and the way he might have looked at an Iowa sky of mounting clouds or New York skyscrapers or the way he lifted a barrel of grease into the bed of a Ford pickup or folded clothes into a box helped me. It made my imagination more elastic. It lightened my conception of metaphor. It rescued me from the riddles of my own life. Seeing him in the boxing ring those afternoons in New York—the key, he says, is always to hit the other guy first—taught me to pry into time that's always in motion, to get up from my own life and look into how you got here, to be curious. Not only that, but to see fantasies and memories and dreams and projection in the same way. It was to discover that the world exists in time and across time. And that the patterns of our lives' existences are what exist.

Joe's life was like a dedication to the future. His hours became a part of my own. Winter nights in our room in Brooklyn, we'd be huddled in the middle of the floor trying to stay warm. The air above us hovered too—but, no, he says to me, stop with describing the air. What's the use, he says, why do you do that? A man doesn't live looking for explanations, he says. He was getting up now and gathering his tallis bag for the weeknight service at the shul. He changed into a threadbare dress shirt, a clean blue tie, and a double-breasted blue jacket. Outside, the afternoon light was waning. It might have been November. What about death, I said—we were walking fast now on the sidewalk. It needs explanation, no? Not so lonely as living here, he says. Don't you want to be understood, I asked. And then what, he says. The cold air was dismantling our senses. But death won't forgive, I said. We'd stopped at a corner, and his expression reminded me not to press. He had that kind of look. And when he looked at you with it—a look that says there's a door right in front of you but you'll never learn how to open it, Bub—you knew to stop. It was time for us to go anyway, even as the uncertainties shook with longing and widened the world.

We arrived at shul and settled in. The *Maariv* service opened as always with some warm-up prayers, and Joe was saying them absentmindedly. Once we got to the *Sh'ma*, I seemed to disappear from his consciousness as he reimagined our creation by God who had created the world and gave us the Torah on Mount Sinai. I could hear in his voice a desire for future redemption. It was hard to know where his faith in creation and revelation resided most of the time. But here, in shul, he sang it into identity. For the *Amidah*, I was gone from him entirely. He knew the service by heart from the time he was eight or nine years old attending *cheder* in Cherniostrov. He could be called up for the haftarah and chant it cold. Now his eyes were closed, rocking back on his heels, one hand shoved into his trousers pocket, the other holding up the prayer book, chanting the prayers without looking at the words. Watching him alone among the handful of men whose pilgrimages had begun in places in Eastern Europe where the synagogues would one day be makeshift, where all that remains there would be a water stain form the *mikveh* bath or the echo of dying animals that underwent ritual slaughter, or some smashed relics with Hebrew inscriptions, abandoned gravestones, and who now, these

men of New York, were chanting their praises and grat-
itudes in a grave mumble and daring themselves to be
surprised with living, watching them, I realized then
that we never invited anyone back to our room. Instead
we would meet them only at shul, where, like a heart-
beat, a body stood and sat and stood again.

I'd had the same thought once the summer before. It
was July 4, and we'd gone up to Yankee Stadium for a
doubleheader against the Senators. The first game was
a wipeout. Washington's pitcher, Sloppy Thurston, was
easy pickings for the Yankees' hitters for the opening
four innings. And so Walter Johnson had to hobble out
in the fourth. The Senators' troublemaker in the first
game was Goose Goslin. He picked at Yankees hurler
George Pipgras with three hits. The Yankees' pitcher,
Pipgras, whipped pitch after pitch past the other Senators, for whom it was all swing and a miss at their
end, a lot of called strike threes or weak dribblers to
the infield. We'd come especially to watch this rookie
kid, Pipgras, because he was from Ida Grove, Iowa. The
Yankees scored eight runs by the bottom of the fourth
and then four more in the eighth, and won 12–1. Babe
Ruth and Lou Gehrig each had two hits, with one of
Gehrig's—the pitch had arrived middle in and fat—
belted like a lollipop to the deepest part of center field.
There was so much backspin the white cowhide seemed
to peel right off the ball, and then what was left of the
ball departed the world out of sight behind the fence

when we—all of us—seemed returned briefly to who we actually were.

The second game went worse for the Senators, who lost 21–1. Gehrig slammed another home run, and the Babe, who was three for three in the second game before being taken out midway to get some rest, chopped a triple down the right field line. He hacked the ball, is what he did. You would've thought he was cutting down a tree. The ball ricocheted off his bat, rolled deep into the outfield, and got tangled up in the corner there. You could not have loved a smile so big as the one my grandfather had on his face as he watched the Bambino, like a bathtub on two skinny legs, running and huffing as he rounded second base. When Ruth finally slid into third to beat out the throw, he belly-flopped across the dirt and smothered the flat bag with his chest, holding on to it for a few moments like a boy with a puppy.

Around that time we struck up a conversation with a man in a long black beard who was dressed in dark clothes. He'd been staring at Joe since earlier in the first game with that lopsided grin people get when they think they know you but aren't sure. He asked if Joe was from a town in Russia and said the town's name. I didn't recognize it. No, Joe says, not that town. They talked some about a river, a crossroads, this way to Mykolaiv, that way to Proskurov. They shook hands. And then we all went back to watching the game again, the crowd moving in one useless motion now, delighted with the flashes of genius. Times like those lead you to believe that writing is, before it's anything else, about simply getting it straight. Leaving the stadium together was like leaving the synagogue together. Our little room waited for Joe to return. Ahead were other kinds of promises.

# PRIMAL TALK

Most nights, usually late, after everyone was back in the apartment in Boston on Glenville Ave., friends would wander up into the apartment, too, and the kitchen would become a room of talk. More than a room. It was an arena of talk—of discussion and debate and holding forth. We'd talk about friendships and politics and music, love affairs and readings and lectures and ideas. We read out loud passages from what we'd been studying and then talk about those. We'd talk about the neighborhood dogs, Sarge and Lady and Tut. We'd talk about Luba, the Russian seamstress who worked down the street, and Jackie Pepper, the wisecracking waitress at Arthur's Seafood and Deli, another gathering place weekend mornings for late breakfasts of coffee and eggs.

We'd tell stories from the day and from our deep pasts. Here is Paul telling us about the fights that took place after junior high school in Bessie Baker Park in Beverly, up on the North Shore where he grew up. "Bessie Baker,

3:15!" That's what you'd say if you were daring some kid to fight you later in the day after a stare-down during recess. Giff told the story of his little brother, Tucker, on the second floor of their house in Chicago calling down to him in the yard to throw the football up through the open window, and when Giff tossed the ball up—"a beautiful spiral!"—Tucker slammed the window shut so the ball broke through the glass. The Jewish kids in my neighborhood in Houston, well, I would tell them, we'd go walking up Rutherglen along Godwin Park in the mild mid-December nights to steal Christmas light-bulbs from the scattering of non-Jewish houses and smash them in the street because the bulbs made such a pure explosive crack. We'd lob a bulb high into the dark air—"Going Christmas shopping" was what we called it—and wait for it to shatter on the pavement. And here is Nick telling how much he hated his father's nickname for him, Rascal. "Rascal!" the old man would call out to his son in the grocery store in New Jersey when it was time to go and Nick would be playing in the toy aisle. So Nick got his parents to let him get him a dog. And he named the tyke Rascal, and so that way he was never called the name again.

If we couldn't get the others to laugh, the story was a failure. If we couldn't get the conversation to turn phil-osophical, same thing. One thing we never talked about was television. We didn't have one. Proudly we missed out on what was most popular in TV culture during the

1980s. Proudly and sanctimoniously. It's hard to explain how essential we viewed this act. We considered television culture to be crass, a corporate monster that would destroy our brains. Ideas weren't exchanged on television, just flashes of spiritual death. We wanted above all substance, but on TV there was mere celebrity worship and selling beer with sex. Each of us might have given a different reason for why television was forbidden in the apartment, but I suppose its absence meant we wanted to extol the intimate, to be redeemed by living fully in the moment.

Of the four of us who lived at Glenville, I was the most laconic. The others seemed to arrive in the kitchen each night with anecdotes from the day fully formed. When they told stories, they wanted to alter how you saw the world and to confirm some connection with all our desires. The feel of all this talk was like a continuous grand conversation in which one's entire ability to feel or be understood got put into the forefront of your being. Coming in and out of the kitchen those late nights were friends and girlfriends and neighbors. There were An and Jia, the two Cambodian boys in elementary school who lived downstairs with their grandparents, and who liked to sit at the table and do their homework and eat the fruit from the countertop, and listen to the cussing and talk of sex and political debates. Jeff Smith was a regular, stopping over at the apartment several times a day. He'd pace the kitchen with a conspiratorial air as if we were living in Paris during the Occupation. Accompanying him usually was Dayton Marcucci, who had a fondness for dressing as a communist nun and lived in the bell tower of a nearby church. He was Italian and steeped in European history—"You Americans know nothing of Mussolini and his speeches from the balcony at Palazzo Venezia"—and he later moved to Pozzuoli near Naples. Jeff introduced us to Jade Barker. Charlie Weir, Paul's childhood friend, would come down from Beverly with his guitar and sleep on the couch for weeks at a time.

I can close my eyes now and see them all arriving like phantoms: Jim Ditmer, Cindi Rittenhouse, Marlana Thall, Marc Maron, and Andrea Berman. Ted Lukes of Arizona and Gail Whitney of Minnesota and Vicki Halal and Jeff Hall. Laura Cavaluzzo and Mark Lurie and Chris Snell and Brooke Nelson and Laurie Geltman and Adair Peck, whose paintings of orange-faced women we hung on the walls. Gavin and Zoia and Izzy and Shari Katzman and Derek Tomie and Morgan Littlefield. Jamie Greacen and the Miller siblings, Val and Rick. To keep moving in and among all that talk we would juggle. Two of us would grab juggling balls from a basket on the kitchen table and work over our patterns—behind the back, under the leg, four balls at once, and then take to passing six balls back and forth to each other. We'd juggle and talk into the night. All that talk was like juggling too—back and forth tossing the words, trying to lob them so the other person couldn't miss. And on the receiving end you're doing everything you can acrobatically to catch what's sent your way, even from the most erratic throw. We'd throw in and gather up and toss back the talk over and again into the air. We'd scoot one way to stab an errant aside or leap to catch a high one. We'd dive to the ground. We'd play a bad toss off the kitchen cabinet like an outfielder gloving a line drive off the wall.

The pleasure of the talk became its purpose. The two activities of juggling and talking realigned our sensibilities toward affection and gratitude and love and friendship. We made distinctions about everything: the difference between liberalism and progressivism, between John Dewey and Jane Addams, between John Adams and Thomas Jefferson, Grant and Lee, Nixon and Reagan, Bob Marley and Jimmy Cliff and UB40. We talked about growing up and the meanings of names, who we looked up to and what scared us. We talked about our regrets and embarrassments and the craziest thing we'd done over the last three or four days. Did we sing in the shower? Did we believe in God? Did we believe in luck? We made pacts about pulling the plug if one of us became a comatose vegetable. We debated the American dream, whether it was an ethical doctrine, what it said about national identity and individual agency. We celebrated joy. And we did all this while half-baked with cheap weed, while drinking average beer and eating toast and smoking cigarettes. There was talk and more talk. Years of our lives in which our voices were our identities.

In every way these conversations were the practice of finding a voice, of being heard, and of listening. We were becoming artists of interest in the sounds of the mouth, as well as of pleasing each other, of finding all things fascinating. We were infected by talk as if we had happened onto some native language only we knew how to tap into. We were inflamed with words. We wanted each other to hear the soul in speech, what we might be struggling against, what was significant. These were the formative hours of becoming a voice, of learning to make metaphor to delight, to use the words of one experience to tell a story about another experience, to zigzag like starlings with words. Even if the particulars of the conversation are gone now, the identities that were formed from the talk continued within us for years. For me, writing became a way to keep my end of the conversation going. The spirit of the talk was inclusion, communion, belonging.

Only on occasion did someone come into the apartment and make a buzzkill of the talk. Usually it was because they'd be talking over others, stealing the conversation to prove how smart he was, how funny she could be. That's when one of us would crowd the interloper out by getting all appreciative of each of the other three guys who lived at Glenville, of appreciating each other more than the loudmouth. We'd talk about

how at home we felt with each other. We'd start juggling again in the center of the kitchen. We'd begin to
listen to each other exclusively, alert and magnetic to
each other, asking a question to keep the talk between
us. We wouldn't take our eyes off each other—the four
of us in those moments. We would only look at each
others' faces so that the loudmouth could sense that the
one talking was meant to be seen as the most interesting
person in the world. It was unsportsmanlike. But it was
our kitchen. Our primal talk. Later, writing would rep-
licate that process. One of the thrills of being a writer
is becoming aware of the wildness that percolates inside
of you. Writing seeks a form to externalize it. If you've
learned to listen, you're able to hear it. It gets tossed at
you. And you toss it back into words at the world.

One night with about a half dozen friends in the
kitchen, I brought out and read some Ralph Waldo
Emerson I'd been reading for a course in American
literature—

> In good company, there is never such discourse
> between them alone. In good company, the in-
> dividuals merge their egotism into a social soul
> exactly coextensive with the several conscious-
> nesses there present. No partialities of friend to
> friend, no fondnesses of brother to sister, of wife
> to husband, are there pertinent, but quite other-
> wise. Only he may then speak who can sail on the

common thought of the party, and not poorly limited to his own. Now this convention, which good sense demands, destroys the high freedom of great conversation, which requires an absolute running of two souls into one.

And then we went on for an hour talking about companionship and irony and memory. Giff grabbed his coat and headed up to the roof deck to smoke a cigarette, so we followed and left our invisible selves back in the kitchen to carry on with the serious talk about the transcendental. From the roof deck you could see the trees in an autumn breeze above Ringer Park.

A few weeks earlier Jeff Smith and Paul and I and some girlfriends had taken mushrooms and climbed up into those red- and golden-leafed trees like priests wagging our beards. We were hoping to find some antidote to trivializing our lives—that's what we said anyway—and unslaving ourselves from ourselves. Hallucinating in the early evening, we sat atop the thickest branches. It was like their functions no longer had any significance. What I could perceive from there in the haze of hallucination was perception itself detached from the figure and form of the world. To be both inside and outside of nature was to renew meanings and meaninglessness of the living world. Since the appearance of the light and the trees, the park and the city streets, the noise of the traffic and the children playing in the park was no longer limitless, and my awareness of this wild paradise and my ordinary reality became one.

Soon it was just Giff and me on the rooftop. The others threaded back down the stairs to warm up. I was talking about the mushroom trip I'd had in the park, how overwhelming the flood of perception was. I adore the rational, I was saying, the utilitarian. But for survival we need to embody potential experience, I was saying, the primitive with all its possibilities of discoveries. Giff was listening and nodding his head, working his hands over the cigarette. We were both standing now in the city's darkness. The streetlights had come on. What we think is the point, he said finally, is always somewhere else than where it's supposed to be. We've got to postpone our certainty, I said, as all of Boston glowed in the dark. I said, in order to allow the illusion to emerge, to keep what's lost. We can't get reduced to the smallest variant, Giff said back. We were both sitting on the edge of the roof with our feet dangling. Every moment is small and clear and free, I said, and then it's gone. But the sweet faces of the people are still down there, he says. That is what you want to see, I said. Definitely, he said. I definitely want to see that. You're trying to move and not wanting to move, I said. Well we're just acting, Giff said, we're just acting this out for someone else's benefit. I don't think meaning, I said, can be cast aside someday when it's been outgrown.

We went on like that in conversation, effortlessly

moving in step with each other, anticipating the other's next move. We would build on each other's approach, and you wouldn't have known who was leading and who following.

# THE DUGOUT

One afternoon in the Dugout on Comm. Ave. Marc Maron invited me to sit at a table with him. Marc was with a couple of guys from the English department I'd seen around but didn't know. I knew Marc because we had been in a few classes together. Occasionally he'd come by Glenville to talk about his favorite new writers and drink beer in the kitchen, but usually we saw each other in the university or bumped into each other at neighborhood parties of mutual friends. That afternoon the guys were sitting in a booth in the underground bar talking about deconstructionism: Derrida, de Man, Barthes, Lacan. It's the new thing, one of them insisted. Then the conversation turned to politics. I was uneasy because I had become involved in the Mel King mayoral campaign and knew a good deal about the race, but I didn't want to be seen as unserious about literature. So I said something about a poet I was just discovering, Robert Bly. I had just read his first book, *Silence in the Snowy Fields*. In my knapsack I was carrying the Bly book and another book of poems I was reading a lot, and I would poke around in these two books on and off during the day.

Even though *Silence in the Snowy Fields* was published in the spring of 1962, it was the first contemporary book of poetry I'd read with any seriousness. Since I was considering leaving Boston for Vermont after graduation, I took Bly's winter poems about the deep unconscious as a kind of guide to living in the north. Bly, I was saying to the guys at the Dugout, doesn't view life as abstract or accidental. I took a sip of beer and read some lines from one of the poems, "Three Kinds of Pleasure"—

I

*Sometimes, riding in a car, in Wisconsin*
*Or Illinois, you notice those dark telephone poles*
*One by one lift themselves out of the fence line*
*And slowly leap on the gray sky—*
*And past them, the snowy fields.*

II

*The darkness drifts down like snow on the picked*
   *cornfields*
*In Wisconsin: and on these black trees*
*Scattered, one by one,*
*Through the winter fields—*
*We see stiff weeds and brownish stubble,*

*And white snow left now only in the wheeltracks of the combine.*

Of course life is abstract and accidental, Marc interrupted, and that's how our language becomes dogmatic. Dogmatic and structured, another added. I didn't agree but stayed quiet. Though I wasn't really sure. Bly's poems were making me see how the unconscious resists the imposition of external structures, and even resists the aesthetic, instead focusing on the archetypal and on the passages of existence common to everyone. They were unconvinced. One of them spoke about how poetry should be a song of critical thought that should locate a reality devoid of myth in a language no one has ever spoken or heard before, and that it should take itself apart and eliminate from that text the living experience. There's no way to overcome it, another was saying. Like many other English majors of our generation, we had been enlisted to disturb the tranquility of language. We were taught to think further and further away from everyday human experience. Our table in the basement of the Dugout was like a symbol of this battle. Our table would have been depicted only as a representation of how much we were able to face down modernism and that we mustn't be deceived by the illusion of language. The role of reading was to see the insufficiency of language.

I wanted to believe this kind of theorizing. But really I rejected it. And I pitied them for chaining themselves to their generalizations. Language never seemed lost to me, nor the world that it's meant to represent. It was as if these guys had been stood up by reality and so needed to blind themselves with weapons against the language of reality. Their heads were so filled with English department-isms that the small physical and psychic actuality of life was invisible. They still thought of ordinary life as inferior to the symbolic one found in literary criticism. I wanted to be accepted by them but not enough to disconnect my body from the world. And I didn't want to give up the prerogatives of the flesh or the intimacies of imagination; I knew that much even then. I was too suspicious of the detachments of theory anyway. I hungered for what physically gave me pleasure. Language was one of those things.

On this particular afternoon I'd had a couple of beers and was in a swagger. I talked about the Mel King campaign and how we were trying to get Mel elected the first black mayor in Boston's history. You want to see the contrast between the meaning of signs, I was saying, help elect Mel. I finished a beer and ordered another. They didn't know much about Mel. So I told them that he grew up in the South End. His mother was from Guyana and his father from Barbados. In the 1960s he'd been president of Boston's Urban League and worked to get ordinary citizens involved in the development of their own neighborhoods by staging tent-city protests. He'd been a state legislator. Harold Washington and Andrew Young were going to come to Boston and help register voters. I talked about the importance of the new mayor being able to speak the language of the people. It was like knowing the newest dance craze, I said. King is the moonwalk candidate, Marc joked. He was pushing his hair behind his ears and stroking his mustache with his fingers. Right, I said, but not really. King, I said, is the guy who can't get a ticket to the ball. We needed to fight to get him in there. The city's establishment was keeping him out. They were trying to knock him down and kick him and stomp him, I said. They were going to try to leave him bloodied in the street with nothing left but his trousers and a torn shirt. There wasn't going to be any compassion. I felt the guys at the table were listening now, and I made my little play: And out of compassion, I said, comes the true language of democracy, comes a common, moral language, a language of solidarity, of affection and grief and passion and poetry.

The light outside the cellar was darkening by now, and the bar seemed more dimly lit. Along with other upperclassmen there were gathered some professors and business types. In a booth in the corner I recognized some Red Sox players drinking beers and eating the free popcorn. Finally, I came out with it. The Mel King campaign, I said, was the sort of thing Derrida could never avow. You couldn't trust him with such facts of life. But they weren't having any of it. Literature and mayoral politics had nothing in common, one of them insisted, and he began to gather his things. He and Marc took off, and a couple others took off. Still, some of the guys wanted to see what Mel was about. They wanted to see him. It was a Monday night, and I knew Mel was talking at a house party in Allston, so a few of us jumped onto the T and went over to the apartment building. Mel hadn't arrived yet when we got there, so we helped the host with some of the arrangements. When I think about it now, I suppose the rhythm of political meetings made me happy. So much of politics is symbolic speech in the service of the syncopations of the lives we actually live. But the way we gather to vote is with our bodies. It's the dance that goes along with those rhythms. It's like a poem in some ways. The words of political speech are translated into images. And while words refer, images represent. The images are shorthand for an argument. When you think about it, you can see how both political speech and poetic utterance have their origins in life. The soapbox speech and the poem are just two of the ceremonies of life.

Soon the apartment had filled up, and people were lining the stairwell up to the front door. Right about then Mel came in. He had a large face with strong, warm intelligence in his eyes that seemed to arouse everyone in the room. He was staffed by just one guy, a roommate of Jeff Smith's I knew only as Spencer. We said hello and spoke for a minute. Then Mel slipped into the kitchen to make a phone call. He was going to speak in the living room—it had a high ceiling and a balcony. There were no chairs, so everyone was standing. In that room we became a small society of belief that political change was coming. Outside it was already dark. Inside everyone was excited and felt triumphant.

I found a place to sit on the floor near where Mel was going to speak and kept my eyes on his bald black head. I could see he didn't know what to make of the crowd but was appreciative. He looked bemused. And then he started to talk quietly, earnestly, more like a professor in a seminar than one of those happy political warriors. It was like he was doing a verbal dance, elaborately crossing his thoughts and emotions, but with a flourish too in a kind of poetry of community—

I first want to say that nobody does anything on their own. I may stand here as one man, but it's one man who is a compilation of thousands of folks who have been involved in this cause. I just want people to understand that because that's some of the strength of what is happening with this movement. I stand here as a person who's thrilled at what the movement is accomplishing. I have no question or doubts about what the long-range impact is going to come from your work. People talk about the tent city we put together and the importance of people making decisions about what they wanted with the land in their neighborhood. The best things about this campaign is like the best things that happened when students stopped the war in Vietnam. And I think it's important to put it into that perspective. If we are successful here in Boston, others will rise. They'll rise in hundreds and hundreds of cities across this country. That's huge because you're stretching folks by supporting this campaign. If you continue to do that, no telling how far you can go. You have a right to this revolution because we all deserve the best of what is offered in this city.

By now I had given up my spot to a woman in a ponytail who was wearing a blue jean jacket covered in political buttons. The biggest was a blue one that read:

MONDALE/FERRARO.

FOR MASSACHUSETTS.

FOR AMERICA.

I was interested in listening to Mel, and also not. The guys from the Dugout had already left. When Mel was done and worked himself out of the apartment to get to the next house party on his schedule, I too headed downstairs and walked out into the Boston night. I wanted to clear my head. Under a streetlamp I pulled out the copy of the other book I had in my bag, *Out-of-the-Body Travel* by Stanley Plumly, and read a few lines at random before walking back to Glenville—

*I watched you on the wrong side*
*of the river, waving. You were trying*
*to tell me something. You used both hands*
*and sort of ran back and forth,*
*as if to say* look behind you, look out
behind you. *I wanted to wave back.*

After that I couldn't get rid of the conflict about politics and poetry in my mind. I was digging myself into a psychic hole where the political life would call me up and plead with me: I'll carry you, I'll give you energy, I'll fill your hours with citizenship and purpose. And the life of poetry would counter: I'll arouse you, I'll expose your spirit. What I had wanted was to cross over from one world to the other, and when I was in one of the worlds, I then wanted to reenter the other one. At that hour all I could think to do in perfect silence was look at the sky above me with its tiny explosions of stars and open harbors of darkness that we never really see. And then, in the way that images stray into our minds, I thought of the sky above Galveston Island down south of Houston, and a catch of language came into my head that went—

We let our bodies down on the jetty with the
tide high and the dawn light drifting at our feet,
with the waterline's azure palms uncurling and

reaching back. She was a girl I don't remember,
our feet in the gulf water, whiskey, constellations
clenching the hour's teeth.

I fished into my knapsack for a pencil and scrawled
the words into my notebook. And then I wrote down
also something about how I wanted to live next, that I
needed to keep a wildness inside me and mustn't turn
away from the terrors of the underworld.

# SOMETHING'S HAPPENING
# OUT THERE

Taking the Red Line from Central Square to Park Street Station a few days before the November election in 1984 to get to the Mondale rally at the Boston Common, Giff and I started up a lively conversation with a woman carrying a guitar. Like us she was standing up in the crowded subway, but she was dancing as the train swayed over the Charles River. The T bore us away through the monstrous heap of the city, and in the distance you could see the streets of glass-windowed buildings, the brick siding of MIT and BU, facing each other across the river like star-crossed lovers. The weather had been cold, but we were still weeks away from the winter's stretch of blackened snow.

The woman had an ethereal black face and a stunning set of cornrows. She said her name was Tracy. She said she was going to the rally too. She said she had just come back from playing a gig at Nameless Coffeehouse. As the T moved slowly through the two cities of

Cambridge and Boston, we passed the clapboard houses that seemed to me now, in the couple years since I'd left Texas, mysterious and familiar, their high roofs pulled tight like a cap. At the front of one house I could see an older woman shaking out a blanket. She looked up as the T passed, and I wanted to catch her eye. But I didn't. And I could see in her drudgery that she had an exhausted look on her face. Something desolate. Tracy asked what I was looking at. The houses, I said. We got to win this election, Giff said.

At Park Street we all got off with the large crowd. Tracy was suddenly in a rush, and so we headed over separately to the demonstration. Children, couples, students all streaming over and pushing. It was like a city-sized crawl of union workers and leftists and academics and anti-war veterans. When we couldn't get very close to the stage, Giff and I decided to shimmy up a tree and watch the spectacle from there, fifteen feet up, several hundred yards back. The whole mood was festive. The big crowd stretched from the gold-domed State House to Park Street. I had the urgent feeling that we were part of something. That we counted.

From the branches high in the tree you could see a lot of the handmade signs. A lady in a white blouse and a perm raised one and kept swinging and waving it:

RONALD REAGAN, HE'S NO GOOD:
SEND HIM BACK TO HOLLYWOOD!

Another woman in a Fourth-of-July-fireworks-patterned blouse held a sign over head that read: MONDALE WE LOVE YOU. Another: SPEAKS FOR FRITZ.

Hundreds and hundreds of people were holding up the campaign's official red, white, and blue MONDALE FERRARO sign, designed to look like a flag waving in the breeze with a single white star. Lots of people were taking pictures. There were hand-held American flags everywhere. And a long banner on a pole with the words:

RETIRE RONALD REAGAN

All the handmade haiku-like signs made me smile:

NO ONE POLLED US
DON'T LET REAGAN INSULT YOUR
    INTELLIGENCE
MONDALE'S GOT BEEF

That's when we caught sight of Tracy again—she was coming onto the stage now and taking the microphone. It would be a few years until Tracy Chapman had her first album with a song like "Fast Car," and I would never run into her again. But I remember the funny coincidence of seeing her on the T and then onstage—and the husky sincerity of her voice. Then she introduced Peter Yarrow and Mary Travers who came on, and they all led us in a rendition of "This Land Is Your Land." Stephen

Stills came up next and sang "Our House." There was a long, dull break before the local politicians strolled onto the stage, smiling and waving. Giff and I started talking about Whitman and how much he would have adored the spectacle. What's that passage I love, Giff asked, and I quoted the first line to him: "I am of old and young, of the foolish as much as the wise."

Then out came Mondale, flanked by the two senators, Ted Kennedy and Paul Tsongas; the Speaker of the House, Tip O'Neill; and the governor, Mike Dukakis. O'Neill took the microphone first and started getting nostalgic. "The first Democrat I came into Boston to see in 1928," he was saying, "was Al Smith." He says, "I have seen them all. I have seen our own Jack Kennedy. I saw Roosevelt. I saw them, and this rally today reminds me of the week before the election in 1948 when Harry Truman came to Boston. This is exactly what it was like. It was twenty to one. He wasn't going to be president of the United States. Look at this crowd!"

We cheered for ourselves. Now O'Neill was claiming our crowd was ten times larger than the one that turned out for Reagan a few blocks away a few days earlier. He says, "We haven't forgotten compassion in this country!" Then Dukakis was talking: "Something's happening out there that the pollsters just aren't picking up!" There was another wave of cheers. When Teddy Kennedy took the microphone, we swooned. Teddy! Teddy! Teddy! "Ronald Reagan may come to Boston"—Kennedy was in a

Nantucket bellow from the start—"and he may speak in the shadow of the JFK Building, but I only wish he also stood in the light of the principles in which John F. Kennedy believed! Fairness and justice and progress toward peace!" Teddy! Teddy! We chanted.

Other demonstrators were now climbing up the tree Giff and I were in and trying to jostle us out of place. As the crowd cheered Kennedy, he kept up the whip: "And so I've traveled this nation," he was shouting, "and I come home to Boston to say that Ronald Wilson Reagan has no right to quote John Fitzgerald Kennedy!" After Teddy finished, we all started chanting—

We want Fritz! We want Fritz!

Up to the microphone appeared Mondale. He was hoarse, "There's a smell of victory in the air!" We all cheered crazily: "Four more days! Four more days!" Mondale quieted us down. "When Reagan was inaugurated," Mondale was saying, his tired voice cracking, "let history record that the first thing he did when he went into the White House was to take down Harry Truman's portrait and replace it with that great Boston strikebreaker, Calvin Coolidge. Now I make a pledge to you"—he was saying to us, and you could tell he was smiling—"that the first thing I'm going to do is to take down Calvin Coolidge's picture and put Harry's back where it belongs!"

You forgot Mondale's faults in moments like that, and finally he was finishing up by telling us that "Reagan's message to America is that when you're in trouble, you're told you're on your own"—

*If you're unemployed, it's too bad.*
*If you're old, it's tough luck.*
*If you're sick, good luck.*
*If you're black or Hispanic, you're out of luck.*
*I don't believe that for a minute.*
*In America you're not alone!*
*We're all in this together!*

When the rally came to a sudden halt, Giff and I climbed down out of the tree and decided to walk back to Allston. The fall air was sharp and blue. Giff was saying we were going to win, he was sure of it. We were joyful. We were hugging strangers on the sidewalk. But I was saying, wasn't it weird that Mondale was even in Boston just a few days before the election? Didn't the campaign know Boston was going to vote Democratic? I mean, shouldn't he be in Pennsylvania or Michigan?

The coming landslide blindsided us, that's how much we were living in our leftist bubble. Listening to the results a few nights later on the radio in the kitchen at Glenville, surrounded by friends who'd come over to get the returns, I kept turning to the roomful of downcast, saying, Do you know anyone who voted for Mondale? Anyone? Paul and Nick arrived with a couple of six-packs of beer, and we all decided to head up to the roof with a boom box and play some Talking Heads and Prince and UB40. We rushed upstairs and began to roll around up there. Leaning against each other, swinging with the music. There were about a couple dozen of us by now, and people were beginning to arrive even from the street. It was a raucous funereal rebellion of rooftop dancing. One woman was pulling at her hair and shouting, Nancy Reagan is blowing my world! Then she threw her arms around my neck and tried to bite my hand when I attempted to remove her from me. I didn't even know whether she was drunk. Then she let go and collapsed onto the deck, and her face grew calmer.

I made an apologetic bow and headed back downstairs and closed the door to my room. I sat on the bed and tried to relax and looked at my hands. There was a small bruise where she'd bitten me. I felt I was in flux between my mind and the society upstairs, the nation beyond, like I was in a world of fire and some new, original experience. It was something I was going to have to work out for myself. Either I would or I wouldn't, I knew that much. And I knew I didn't have to go far to find it but that I did have to go to where there was some solitude. If it took courage to face this trial of the spirit and to bring a whole new understanding of my experiences, then that was just going to have to be the deed I had to pay. All I could have said then was that I was in need of a single intention.

I thought to try to write for a little while in my

notebook, but it was impossible to find my mind. Anyway I knew I'd need some time to reflect about the last few days and Reagan's landslide reelection. So I just wrote down some words from a poem by Whitman in my notebook—

*I am the poet of commonsense and of the*
    *demonstrable and of immortality;*
*And am not the poet of goodness only . . . . I do not*
    *decline to be the poet of wickedness also.*

And then I left the notebook on my bed. I was sure I was needed elsewhere.

# THE PALE OF VERMONT

After I left Boston for Vermont in the summer of 1986, I thought that now, at last, I would have my own life. I felt like a man who goes to Europe to find himself. But instead I was going into the woods. Fewer than forty-five people lived in Brownsville at the foot of Mount Ascutney when Giff and I leased a small house on a hundred acres and took a couple of teaching jobs in the public schools. I had a romantic feeling about moving to rural New England. Like Henry David Thoreau who, when asked why he never traveled much outside Massachusetts, replied, "I have traveled widely in Concord," I was intent to travel widely in Brownsville. I was intent to have my discoveries, to learn "by my experiment: that if one advances confidently in the direction of his dreams, and endeavors to live the life which he has imagined, he will meet with a success unexpected in common hours." I went to the woods because I too wished to live deliberately—"to front only the essential facts of life, and see if I could not learn what it had to teach, and not, when I came to die, discover that I had not lived."

Going to Vermont I saw myself as someone who was leaning into his youth. I wanted to be at the beginnings of something—and I could hardly imagine what a life would be like without such an ambition. To someone who hasn't lived like that it's almost impossible to describe what it's like. Brownsville was filled with fortunes. There were the natural delights of every season and to every plant and tree and blade of grass. Each curving dirt road was an invitation to meander. The old hills and fields longed for nothing in particular, and the crooked stone walls held on to some broken steadiness of standing still. The walls seemed to have no memory of the farm they were meant to surround even. And the skies were usually full of wind that carried with it a loneliness that felt familiar. The wind came to me and turned back and came again like birds or like the foliage or like remembering the right way home. For a time every fence post brought me to some new emotion. As would the first buds on the apple trees, passing nights with a slender moon, red and gold leaves unveiling a skeleton of a tree against the coming weather, the blurring of autumn colors into long snows, then the longer nights where the fields crawled into a bright freeze, and then a day and another of heavy snow, and days more of the passing whiteness. And the air smelling of woodsmoke.

Anatole Broyard says that to look back at one's youth

is like looking back at some "medieval town in France or Italy and trying to visualize the life of its inhabitants in the thirteenth century." You can remember only isolated, unexpected, uninterrupted images. My first efforts to write in Vermont involved learning how to split open my consciousness, is what I remember. I was still one person, but I felt I had to open myself in order to get around whatever I'd always felt forbidden to do. To get around how I might censor myself or punish myself for thinking and feeling. I felt as if I had fractures in my unconsciousness and that each zone of my self had some difficult urge. I set up a writing desk in a room overlooking the charming, desolate, wooded acres so deep beyond my vision I might as well have been back in the Pale of Settlement in Cherniostrov before my great-grandfather Harry Borg came to America. My view now was the dappled stone hills sloping toward the house in velvet, green waves. At night the stars would dot my imagination, stitching together words I longed to write down.

Nothing can tell you what it was like to be so alone as a writer. And to start writing I knew I had to be. Not that I was entirely alone. Moving to Vermont with Giff gave us years of new adventures, not least of which was our amusing run-ins with Ralph, the town constable. Built the size of a bar, he was ex-Marine, and during our first week there in the early fall, a couple of nights before school started, he chased us off the only road in town because we were standing on it, about forty yards apart, throwing a Frisbee. "No throwing objects across the highway," he said from behind a half-lowered tinted window in his brown sedan. "Even to each other?" we asked. But win us over Ralph did the following spring-time on Town Hall Meeting Day when he requested a bulletproof vest. How many times, someone asked, have you been in a life-threatening situation, Ralph, in the decades you've been the town constable? Ralph approached the microphone near the stage, hitched his belt up over the barn doors of his tucked-in gut, and said in a serious Yankee mumble, "Only takes once," before we all voted, unanimously, to give him the requested protective gear.

I liked his superstitiousness. And I was learning, too, that to become a writer I needed at least to learn about my own superstitions. I needed to commit heresies. And those acts had to feel pleasurable. At first the writing was clumsy, tormented, and hair-raising. The very idea of writing was a physical joy as much as it was a psychic one. It was like discovering another person's body for the first time, naked and striking and flowing in time. I was hungry for archetypal fantasies as much as sexual ones. My sense of myself as a physical being aware of the cadences and idioms of my body had been a long chain of events that led to my arrival at that desk.

But to do so, I can see now, I had to live on a distant road like Route 44 in Brownsville in the county of Windsor. I had to live far removed from the bright streets of my East Texas upbringing. It was like I was taking revenge against my life. I might as well have been living in a foreign movie much less a foreign country. Still there had to be affection and love, too. Word by word, phrase by phrase, line by line, I was un-despairing myself into the love of writing poems. Which was, for me then, like the love of love itself. Like most beginning writers I hadn't learned how to translate boredom or desire. I hadn't learned how to just be with words, to exist near poems with a high degree of comfort with uncertainty. My sense of formality, learned in my studies of poetry in college as much as in my private readings, made it difficult for me to be natural in a poem. For a while I was just acting in my poems. I was guilty about that, too, like I was using models to dress up into my own consciousness. I hadn't realized yet how elemental imitation was. I was constantly disappointed in what I was able to write and say.

I suppose what I was searching for and not finding, perhaps lacking, was how to undress as a writer. And then how to dress in the conscience that was my inheritance. My poems were a kind of wardrobe that was startlingly unfamiliar. But all along I knew I was supposed to be trying to strip the clothing off. I would assemble and disassemble my poems. I would cut up stanzas, literally cut them up with scissors into strips and try to rewrite the strips. Dozens and dozens of little strips of paper littered my desk that offered me, in that remote Vermont room, a view out onto the watery-like acres of lapsed farmland and woodland. The scraps of paper lay on the desk like marooned houseboats piled up alongside a river.

It is almost impossible for people who don't write to understand how much gratification I took from all that failure. When I started to write I only knew how to make guttural sounds, and these I felt I was copying from the past. Style and idiosyncratic little maneuvers I used in place of honest thought and feeling. I disassociated my inner life from the skills I was carving out from other poets in the books I kept at my desk. They gave me their most intense, unmitigated secrets, and I spilled them into my repressed poems. I would plead with those books by Yehuda Amichai and Tomas Tranströmer and Seamus Heaney and Yves Bonnefoy to show me how to get my poems to open up to me. And I could hear my poems pleading back to me to be patient. I was lit up with lust for my writing. I was practically lecherous, enraptured, ravenous. In the process of pleading with my poems, I thought I was trying to present or reveal a better person. That my interior world was better than who I was as a man in the living world. If not better, then purer. What an effort it took! And how willingly and freely I made it.

I remember one night, a frozen February night, alone in the house, and the snow falling for hours, I was writing in the darkness with a single lamp shining over my desk. I was writing as if I were running a straight line into a dream, running for miles and miles even as the snow fell. My energy that night was limitless—a joyous, unspent energy that was created out of writing. I felt covered in doubt, of course, but ennobled too. On my desk was a passage by William Wordsworth from *The Two-Part Prelude*. It was a passage I understood that generations of poets had underlined before me, and so it made me feel connected to the arc of poetry in English:

> *I might advert*
> *To numerous accidents in flood or field,*
> *Quarry or moor, or 'mid the winter snows,*
> *Distresses and disasters, tragic facts*
> *Of rural history that impressed my mind*
> *With images, to which in following years*
> *Far other feelings were attached, with forms*
> *That yet exist with independent life*
> *And, like their archetypes, know no decay.*
> *There are in our existence spots of time*
> *Which with distinct pre-eminence retain*
> *A fructifying virtue, whence, depressed*
> *By trivial occupations and the round*
> *Of ordinary intercourse, our minds*
> *(Especially the imaginative power)*
> *Are nourished, and invisibly repaired.*

I longed for that kind of nourishment, to have my mind impressed with life. I wrote only with this aspect in mind without concern for sense or arrangement.

Writing like this was almost better than later, when I was able to explain to myself what it was I had in mind to do. It was an extreme form of inspiration. Perhaps writing is most pleasurable when it preserves some of that unknowableness that you feel in the beginning, when you're a little frightened and jubilant and fired up with your absurd, quixotic love of words and the white spaces between them, when you are in love with the physical formation of the letters themselves, and you can feel released from the living world. Writing always went badly when I tried to define the terms of the moment, like what was this poem going to mean and why was I writing it? And because I never knew how to puzzle out the answers to those questions, I would try to make them up. And so my writing would begin with a lie. As I pressed up against my ideas of writing, as I felt its fevers and shuddered against its glow, the literary overtook the honest. But then I would carry the images and words from the poems with me everywhere into my daily life as if I were responsible for carrying civilization. My little metaphors were always on my mind. Each one a new object I hauled all over the days and nights like an unwieldy ornament. But I didn't know what to do with them, so I felt like I needed to look away. Then I would peek back at them like a voyeur of my own imagination.

I used to imagine that my poems would then apologize to me for not living up to my expectations. Their lines too long. Their words too Latinate. Their metaphors too thin or too fat. Their meanings too acrid or furtive, insidious or guileless. And so I wavered around my poems. I hovered over them. I read them aloud, talking to myself, mumbling, syllable by syllable, the doomed words keeping me awake, puncturing the silence of the woods. Counting the syllables on my fingers and saying the words out loud, I was like a man all alone in a house talking to himself in a language it seemed no one would ever understand.

But then one poem began to stand out. It was in the springtime. All this writing was, it seemed to me at least, beginning to enter a new kind of idiosyncrasy. I was starting to understand the coral structures of a poem. This one poem had an aquatic vibrancy to it. I could hear it in my heart for days separate from other poems, separate from other events in my life, as if it were lapping against a shore nearby. The poem was like an easy tide coming in and out of being. And then the poem began to get away. It started to become relentlessly rhetorical and began to float away entirely. In the zone of time that the poem began to depart from me, what I was left with was a sad silence. At first I was dogged about it and then sullen. Followed by hopefulness, discretion, and then a plain silence of curiousness. The silence got colder like a burbling stream. It was the kind of silence that can depress a writer. I did everything I could to avoid it. But the silence didn't go away, and yet I was determined not to be judged by it. Still, it vibrated in me. And there was nothing I could do to let go of it all. Surely this is what restlessness means for a writer. An inability to become natural and relaxed with the language, and so nothing could survive.

But then something broke. You could say the soul of the poem arrived. All along, to my surprise, it had been there but outside the poem. I drove back to the place a few towns over where the impulse to write that poem had first taken hold of me. It was a little inconvenient since the source of the poem was a small cluster of flowers I'd seen up the road fifteen miles or more away. The likelihood of the flowers still being there was small. What I'd seen was my first mountain laurel of the springtime—miniature white petals like umbrellas with static, pink strips. I hadn't been looking for anything at all when I'd noticed them before, and for a time I was just confused by it. But I felt an excitement over the discovery, and then a tension, and it was hard to differentiate the two feelings from each other. It was like watching waves somersault into the shoreline from a distance, and trying to distinguish each wave from the next. Like words.

But when I arrived at the spot the laurel was gone. I wandered around by the road as if on a hunt for something that might be like the flower, charming and pink. I was extremely alert, and there was something deeply satisfying in my looking for the old inspiration, something graceful really. It felt like I was in the spirit of recollection. Everything about it, moment to moment, was familiar, tangible, pregnant, fructifying. Nothing about the moment was routine. The disturbances of my past were like a dying bird, and all I could do was figure it out as I went. Right then the poem I was after became a kind of embodiment of significance. And I wrote something while standing on the side of the road, just a few lines as a metaphor of my experience—

> *I found a chimney swift by mountain laurel along*
> *the road*
> *Dying. I tried to shake a breath out of the beak but*
> *no*
> *Air was left. What remained?*

These lines would become the makings for the first poem I published. It was as if I was learning about myself that, in some mysterious way, words had never been static things for me. I moved through them physically. Metaphysically, they moved through me. I wrote them down in the present moment—in a notebook, at my desk—and yet doing so let me travel to something hidden like some unknown future. The reason words offer themselves to this kind of experience so easily rests in the physical nature of phrases and clauses, lines and sentences and stanzas. To write is to uncover, to recover, what the words are hiding. The immediate shapes of letters are like a thicket into a nearby wood. And beyond every thicket of words I might select in order to construct a poem, beyond every thicket of phrases or stanzas, are the ghosts and shadows of all those poems I did not.

But first I had to drive home and sit down at the desk and type up my lines for the poem. When I was done and had placed the paper with the poem on it in a drawer, I leaned back from the desk a little. No one was around. The early afternoon sunlight seemed altogether old-fashioned. The hills and woods in the back of the house survived there like a kind of continuous life, the shadows preserving some ancient memory of shoemakers and tailors, of gathering in a distant town to shop for salt and sugar and matches and kerosene, of waiting for the peddler to arrive from over the hilltop with his wagon of used rags and second-hand suits and copper pots and pans. I wonder what I could possibly have been thinking at that moment. That decisions taken privately begin with alertness to pain and suffering? That my ambition to write meant I wasn't trying to understand the meaning of life but just to experience moments of my existence? That before I took up the journey to write I had to believe that to write meant I was willing to make changes in my life as a result of becoming a writer? That I knew writing might be bad for me, even dangerous? That to change my life I would have to change my knowledge of language? That to become a writer meant asking less of the world, not more?

I leaned forward again and reached over to the desk

to pick up a strip of paper with a few stray lines on it. The paper was about the size of a shirt tag. I crossed out a word and then another so that I could draw myself deeper into the depths of the letters. I could have licked the blue ink.

# THE SUIT

want to give you a suit, my grandfather said to me one morning in his home on the east side of Tulsa. Come into the closet over here. I was visiting from Vermont during my first winter. He was nearly eighty and handsome, still dark-haired with only specks or threads of gray. He was saying I needed a suit because he was sure I wouldn't take the time to buy one. We were the same height and build, though he had thirty pounds on me.

I know what kind of a suit—he paused to make a joke—suits you. Something from Brooks Brothers. We walked into the closet together. There were about two dozen suits hanging neatly on the rod, and he began sliding his hand across the shoulders of each one and moving them up and down the rack. Blue, he says. You could use a blue one. He invited me to touch them and to pull down any of the blue ones that I was interested in. I ran my hands over the fabric of each one. Each suit had a kind of simplicity against the feel of my hands that implied a sophistication that I didn't understand. It was as if each suit—whether worsted or wool or silk—possessed its own brand of inner peace, a capacity to receive and be thankful, and a mystery too beneath their surfaces to shine with some sublime honor. They were tailored, and that gave them each a magnificent elegance. Usually I wore blue jeans and a T-shirt with a suit vest and a corduroy coat, and I affected a nonchalance about clothes. I had an inkling that the purpose of dressing well was to make a statement. But I knew too that elegance came when you forgot what you were wearing. I could feel how touching his suits was like touching different textures of modesty. I think my grandfather—though he wouldn't have put it this way—thought a good suit provided a kind of sex appeal. It made you look snappy. If not that, then it was a sign of good manners, even power. He was a "clothes make the man" kind of man.

The closet was small, and we kept bumping into each other. Lined up on the floor were dress shoes and loafers. On a high shelf next to a stack of boxes was a baseball I knew to be signed by Joe DiMaggio. There was a shoehorn propped up in the corner and, next to it, my great-grandfather's walking cane that I understood my grandfather would use when the time came. Golf tees were scattered on a countertop. He was telling me a complicated story about a time after the Second World War in the late 1940s when he and my grandmother were having breakfast at a deli on one of their trips from Oklahoma to New York. At the deli there was a young fellow who kept looking at him from across the restaurant. And finally, he says, this young fellow walks over to me and says, Are you a Borg? Well turns out the fellow is from Cherniostrov, too, he says. That's right, he says, and the fellow tells me some cousins are still there. They'd left during the war but came back.

One of the things I was trying to do in those days when I was living in Vermont and first starting to write was to think about what motivated people to say the things they said. I was wondering if the memory of that New York City encounter in the deli was like a hum in his brain, building and building over the years, mounting and then descending again, like a dream of flying. I might have asked him about it, but he keeps talking about the deli. He's full of details about the deli. He talks about the steamy display cabinets and all the shouting like someone's about to die. He describes the trays of pickled herrings and dried fish and salted meats. The pastrami and cream cheese and bagels. The little gherkins and onions and lox and the aroma of coffee. There's no white bread in there, he says. That's right, who gets pastrami on white bread? And then he's talking about half-empty ketchup bottles balancing on the tables.

Except for a few stories about his days boxing when he was young or playing baseball, my grandfather liked most to tell the story of his coming to America with his mother and brother and meeting his father in Iowa. Sparse details were his genius. There was the escape in the night and sneaking onto the boxcar. There were the clothes on our back and stealing a piece of bread. He loved presenting everyone as an interesting character, and they each got a nickname like something out of Chekhov: the Cossack, the Bootlegger, the Grocer, the Mohel. Hearing him talk about his great journey to America was always fun. There was nothing in his telling that was too burdensome or self-conscious—we snuck out at night, we carried a featherbed and two silver candlesticks, we left Cherniostrov, we arrived in Lviv, after New York we took a train, and then we got to Iowa. His language was simple. His technique was direct. The materials of his stories had an elegance on the inside and the outside. Serendipity was the grease for the plot. There was malice in the world, his stories told you, but there was good timing too. There was the shake of luck and the beneficence of God. His stories externalized their events for the purpose of the story alone. Details remained obscure except for the most decisive components. But thoughts and feelings were left out, and his stories never told you anything about a landscape or geography. They took place in his voice more than in a landscape—the train took days, we waited for two weeks. He saw no need to describe a street or a tree. You've seen one tree, you seen them all, he was fond of saying. It was as if he understood that the authentic must begin in the voice. And through the texture of the voice—its moral and psychological claims—sensory details emerge with absolute authority.

His interest seemed simply to tell an effective version of his life, to bring only pertinent parts into relief and leave the others unexpressed. The result was that his stories directed you to more questions. You were left looking for the necessary interpretation, and simply preoccupied with the meaning of the sequence.

In the closet we kept touching the suits, and I was reluctant to choose one. My grandfather held up one of the suits at last. I looked at it like a blind man. This one is for you, he says. I stepped out of the closet for a minute, and when I came back in I had the suit on. He walked over to me and buttoned the jacket and told me to turn up the cuffs at my ankles. He led me to a long mirror in the bedroom. I was standing straight with my hips flat and my shoulders sloped forward, and squeezing the muscles at the base of my back. The collar fit under my hair, and my body seemed smoothed out like a bedspread in a hotel. You could do with a trim, he says, touching my hair where it fell over my ears.

In moments like that, putting on the suit, I can now see the spiral arms of one experience moving outward and away at a great speed, while elsewhere the spirals of a remembered experience are moving inward to the interior of being. On the one hand, there is a movement toward the formal, while on the other hand there is an immersion into the intuitive where, as in a garden, grieving is nurtured. That year Halley's comet could be seen, and I was curious about this bubble falling through space and the way it comes again and again regardless of what we did or didn't do in history or even in our lives. And I want to believe that all of that—the memory as much as the imagination of it—is no different from the light and darkness of my own body.

He had spun me around to face him now and was raising and lowering my arms and then adjusted the jacket over my shoulders. I was gazing directly into his eyes as if we were in a crowded train and we're passing through the little towns and there's a taste of salt in the air and a bony balance in the trees and beyond that the expanse of time. I focused on the crinkles around his eyes like tracks in the snow. His eyes withheld their mysteries, as if he'd traveled into and out of some forest.

Turn around again, he says, let me see the back. I did as he asked and could feel him standing behind me now, close, as if about to whisper into my ear, as if he's going to say something about cocking my fists, about starting with the back and shoulders and then where to put my feet, the front of his knees almost pressed against the backs of my knees as he's whispering again. He runs his hands over my shoulders again and says quietly, more to himself than to me, It's a good suit.

# ACKNOWLEDGMENTS

To give proper due to all whom I owe gratitude for this book, and the life from which it came, would result in one of those obscene catalogues you see nowadays. I'm going to restrict myself to close comrades.

For five years of working with Brian Spears, my editor at *The Rumpus*, he has used his acumen to shepherd my writing far more than I deserve. Though I don't make it easy for him, he has valiantly labored to keep me from alienating readers. When I have caused controversy, the fault has been entirely mine. This book is dedicated to him. Thanks also to the tireless staff at *The Rumpus*. Some of what appears in this book first appeared there.

No amount of thanks is enough to Dinah Lenney. Gratitude to Dan Smetanka at Counterpoint Press for his guidance and friendship and gifted booksmanship, and to the entire, wonderful staff. This book is the first of mine brought to you by Counterpoint, a publishing house I have admired for decades.

Michael Collier, Jim Heynen, and Stanley Plumly—

fine literary men—are due deep gratitude for offering to read this book and to tell me my business, which I desperately needed to hear.

The reasons to thank Rick Gifford, Paul Ruest, Nick Keller, and Jeff Smith are countless. As are the thanks. No value can be placed on our friendship. They have been invaluable in helping me put it all in order, which is akin to helping me stay alive.

Thanks to Anatole Broyard for the inspiration, and to everyone mentioned and alluded to inside this book.

Love and gratitude to Wendy Willis for being smart and wise and joyful and full of love—and to the full catastrophe of the Crow's Nest near and far.

DAVID BIESPIEL is the author of *A Long, High Whistle*, a collection of pieces drawn from his long-standing column in *The Oregonian* about writing and poetry that won the 2016 Oregon Book Award for General Nonfiction. He has also written five books of poetry, most recently *Charming Gardeners* and *The Book of Men and Women*, which was named one of the Best Books of the Year by the Poetry Foundation and received the 2011 Oregon Book Award for Poetry, and a book on creativity, *Every Writer Has a Thousand Faces*. He is the editor of the Everyman's Library edition of *Poems of the American South* and *Long Journey: Contemporary Northwest Poets*, which received the PNBA Book Award. He writes the Poetry Wire column for *The Rumpus*. Among his honors are a National Endowment for the Arts Fellowship in Literature, a Wallace Stegner Fellowship, and a Lannan Fellowship. He lives in Portland, Oregon, with his family.